YOUR IRISH ANCESTORS

YOUR IRISH ANCESTORS

A Guide For the Family Historian

IAN MAXWELL

Pen & Sword
FAMILY HISTORY

First published in Great Britain in 2008 by
PEN & SWORD FAMILY HISTORY
an imprint of
Pen & Sword Books Ltd
47 Church Street
Barnsley
South Yorkshire
S70 2AS

ISBN 978-1-84415-789-1

A CIP catalogue record for this book
is available from the British Library

Typeset in 11/13pt Erhardt by
Concept, Huddersfield

Printed and bound in England by
CPI UK

*Pen & Sword Books Ltd incorporates the Imprints of Pen & Sword Aviation,
Pen & Sword Maritime, Pen & Sword Military, Wharncliffe Local History,
Pen & Sword Select, Pen & Sword Military Classics, Leo Cooper,
Remember When, Seaforth Publishing and Frontline Publishing.*

For a complete list of Pen & Sword titles please contact
PEN & SWORD BOOKS LIMITED
47 Church Street, Barnsley, South Yorkshire, S70 2AS, England
E-mail: enquiries@pen-and-sword.co.uk
Website: www.pen-and-sword.co.uk

Contents

Abbreviations

GO	Genealogical Office
HC	House of Commons
LC	Local Custody
LDS	Latter Day Saints
NAI	National Archives of Ireland
NLI	National Library of Ireland
PRONI	Public Record Office of Northern Ireland
RAI	Royal Irish Academy
RCB	Representative Church Body
UHF	Ulster Historical Foundation

INTRODUCTION

R everence for deceased relatives is common throughout the world. It is one of human history's oldest and most basic religious beliefs. It has been extensively documented in Africa, East Asia and the Pacific. In general, ancestors are believed to wield great authority, having special powers to influence the course of events or to control the well being of their relatives. They can communicate with the living through dreams and by possession. The attitude to them is one of mixed fear and reverence. If neglected, the ancestors may cause disease and other misfortunes.

In Ireland the attitude to ancestors is, to say the least, more ambiguous. The Roman historian Tertullian recorded that the Celts used to sleep on the graves of their ancestors to obtain wisdom. Today, family historians content themselves with recording gravestone inscriptions, and not in expectation of wisdom but a sense of continuity with the past. They are motivated by the need to preserve the memory of their ancestors for future generations.

Family history in Ireland has, in recent years, become an increasingly popular pastime. It is the fact that Ireland was one of the first countries to evolve a system of hereditary surnames that makes it possible to trace the history of even the most humble of families. Genealogy has, however, developed from lists of names in a family tree to a more comprehensive study of the lives of our ancestors. The dedicated family historian will be interested in more than where and when people lived but also their lifestyle, how historical events impacted on their lives and how the family circumstances changed over the generations. This often requires – or leads to – knowledge of antique law, old political and administrative boundaries, folk customs and traditions, and political and social history.

A large number of Irish genealogy books are already on the market. This book will differ from other Irish ancestor books in that the first half will take the form of a detailed social history showing how the lives of our ancestors changed over the centuries and how this is reflected in the records that have survived. It will help family historians put their ancestral research in historical perspective, giving them a better under-standing of the world in which their ancestors lived.

The second half of the book details the more important record collections and where they can be found. Many, like the early twentieth-century census returns and school registers, will be familiar to researchers. Others, like Boards of Guardian records and Grand Jury records have been traditionally overlooked by all but the most experienced of genealogists.

Above all, it aims to generate interest in the absorbing subject of family history. But be warned, part of the pleasure of this most fascinating pastime is that one can never close the book on the lives of our ancestors. After years of searching it only takes one fresh clue to begin the search afresh!

Chapter 1

BIRTH, DEATH AND MARRIAGE

Of the more than eight million people who lived in Ireland at the eve of the Great Famine, records of only a small percentage have survived. The landless labourers who walked the roads in search of work, the subtenant who leased his small plot of land from middlemen, the navvies who built the canals and railways, the pedlars and the destitute survive in few records: the destruction of the nineteenth-century census returns has consigned many in the first half of the nineteenth century to oblivion. Only with the introduction of full civil registration in the mid-1860s can we hope to locate our ancestors with any degree of certainty. More than eight hundred years of history, however, would make life difficult for the hard-pressed registrar in Ireland.

It was not until 1 January 1864 that the state took responsibility for the registration of all births, marriages and deaths in Ireland. This was nearly thirty years later than similar legislation was passed in England and Wales, and ten years after Scotland. Provisions had been made from the 1 April 1845 to enable the registration of non-Catholic marriages in Ireland and for the appointment of registrars who were also given the power to solemnize marriages by civil contract. In addition, the post of Registrar General of Marriages was created and given responsibility for the central collection and custody of marriage records. These provisions, based on the

Author's grandfather and grandmother, c *late 1930s.*

legislation introduced in England and Wales, empowered the Established Church to register marriages in Anglican churches but marriages in other churches were to be registered by a civil registrar. In Ireland the Roman Catholic Church was concerned that this latter requirement might detract from the religious nature of the marriage ceremony and they were consequently excluded from the legislation.

Over time, demand grew for a general registration system of births, deaths and all marriages. The lack of a comprehensive system in Ireland was having repercussions in Britain where many Irish emigrants had gone in search of work. The growing number of laws regulating factory employment, public health conditions and rights of inheritance made it increasingly necessary for people to prove such things as their age and legitimacy. In 1854, for example, the Inspector of Factories for Scotland reported great difficulty in the operation of the Factory Acts because of the large number of young Irish emigrants presenting themselves for employment with fictitious 'birth certificates'. By hiring young Irish labourers, factory owners were getting around the legal ban on employing young persons under 18 years to look after machinery required to be kept in motion during the night.

Pressure for the compulsory recording of births, deaths and marriages in Ireland reached its peak in the mid–Victorian period. Members of the Presbyterian community complained that the absence of this facility made it very difficult to establish rights of inheritance and noted that those of its members seeking commissions in the Indian service could not show proof of their age or origins. The Irish Poor Law Commissioners were also finding it very difficult to impose compulsory vaccination against smallpox because of the absence of information about births and deaths. Eventually, in 1863, a Bill providing for the registration of births and deaths in Ireland was introduced and passed. Whilst the Act did not encompass Catholic marriages, a Private Members Bill was successfully introduced later that year which resulted in the civil registration by the state of marriages celebrated according to the rites of the Catholic Church, ensuring a complete Irish civil registration system was at last in place.

Although registrars were responsible for the actual registers themselves and for their safe-keeping, the legal obligation to register births, deaths and marriages rested with the public. This legal obligation was backed by heavy fines for failure to register. Nevertheless, although there was a fine of £1 for the wilful neglect to register a birth, frequent examples of applicants for old-age pensions in the 1930s and 1940s who found it difficult to establish their claim suggests that many births were not recorded in the 1860s and 1870s.

Non-registration was only one problem. In 1901, Registrar General, Sir Robert E Matheson published the second edition of his *Varieties and Synonymes of Surnames and Christian Names in Ireland*, for the guidance of registration officers and the public in searching the indexes of births, deaths and marriages. He commented:

> *None but those actually engaged in registration work can have an idea of the practical difficulties which are encountered by persons searching the Indexes, owning to the great variations in names in Ireland. These variations are not only in spelling and form, but entirely different names are used synonymously by the same person or by members of the same family.*

Ireland was one of the first countries to evolve a system of hereditary surnames. They emerged during the eleventh century. As the population increased and more than one person with the same name lived locally it became necessary to have a more precise identification. At first the surname was formed by prefixing Mac (meaning son of) to the father's Christian name or O (meaning grandson) to that of a grandfather or earlier ancestor. Many people believe that the Mac is a sign of Scottish origin. However, names like MacMahon, MacGuire, MacNamara and MacCarthy are essentially Irish names. Later names were formed by the occupation of the father, as for example Mac an Bhaird, son of the bard (modern Mac Ward and Ward) or O hIceadha-icidhe, doctor or healer (modern Hickey). Sometimes the name denoted a particular feature or peculiarity of the grandfather or father such as Mac Dubhghaill, black stranger (modern MacDowell). On other occasions a nickname was incorporated such as Mac an Mhadaidh-mada, meaning dog (now MacAvaddy).

The introduction of the English language and the fact that legal and official documents were often prepared by clerks who had no knowledge of the Irish language complicated matters. Names were often anglicized to a form in English that was close to the sound of the Gaelic. Therefore O Dubhthaigh became O'Duffy and then Duffy. Also rare names were often absorbed by better known ones of somewhat similar sound, for example, Sullahan changed to Sullivan. It was not until the advent of compulsory national education and official registration during the nineteenth century that some kind of stability came to the spelling of surnames.

Irish registrars therefore faced considerable difficulties with the large number of variations in surnames presented to them. As Matheson pointed out, the registration of births, marriage and deaths quickly revealed considerable variation in spelling and use of surnames due to local dialect, pronunciation and inconsistency in spelling until well into the nineteenth century. In his *Special Report on Surnames in Ireland*, published in 1909, Matheson includes numerous examples of variation in the spelling of surnames which depended upon the whim of the holder.

> *Some years ago the marriages of a brother and of a sister in the same family were solemnized in a Registrar's office. The son gave his surname as 'Faulkner' and his father's surname as 'Faulkner'. The daughter gave her surname as 'Falconer', and her father's surname as 'Falconer'. Both marriages were subsequently re-solemnized in a place of worship, and the same name orthographical differences were found to exist in the records kept by the officiating minister.*

Before the development of civil registration, genealogists and solicitors made great use of the census returns for Ireland to prove family relationships. The first properly organized census in Ireland commenced in 1813, but this was never completed due to inexperienced enumerators and a traditional hostility to government officials means that figures produced by the census are open to dispute. Dr James Doyle, Bishop of Kildare and Leighlin, declared in 1813 that:

> *The Catholics have every been unwilling to make known their numbers to any agent of the Government. Having too often experienced from it what they deemed treachery or injustice they naturally distrusted whomsoever approached them in its name. Ignorant of its views in computing the number of its slaves, these latter rather feared they were to be decimated or banished, as if in the time of Cromwell, to some bog or desert if found too numerous, than that any measures were to be adopted for the improvement of their condition.*

From 1821, the year of the next census, relations between the government and the people had improved sufficiently for the Catholic clergy to encourage members of their church to give accurate information. From 1841 the heads of households were supplied with forms on which to make returns, a method thought to be 'less intrusive than requiring it to be filled by the enumerator from viva voce inquiry'. The returns were held by the Public Record Office (now National Archives) in Dublin. According to the 28th *Report of the Deputy Keeper of the Public Records in Ireland*, 1896, the census material was proving invaluable to those engaged in ancestral relationship:

The Census Returns of 1813, 1821, 1831–34, 1841 and 1851, are of record here transferred at different times from their places of original deposit. Their accessibility to the public has proved of incalculable value in inquiries concerning title and pedigree and the tracing of next-of-kin and heirs-at-law.

It therefore was an immeasurable disaster when the census records before 1861 were destroyed during the Irish Civil War in 1922 and those from 1861–91 were pulped by government order into waste paper during the First World War.

From 1922, therefore, genealogists interested in details of births, marriages and deaths before full civil registration in 1864 have been forced to search through the registers of individual churches for evidence of their ancestors. From 1537 until 1870 the Church of Ireland was the state church in Ireland. There was a legal obligation for the Church of Ireland to keep records from 1634, although many rural parishes did not start to keep detailed records until the middle of the eighteenth century. Nevertheless, as a general rule, the records of the Church of Ireland start much earlier than those of other Protestant denominations and of the Roman Catholic Church.

Before 1782 it was not legal for Presbyterian ministers to perform marriages. In 1704, some Presbyterians residing at Lisburn were excommunicated by the Episcopal authority for the crime of being married by ministers of their own church. For this reason many marriages of other denominations, especially those classed as Dissenters, are recorded in the Church of Ireland registers. In 1840, the Armagh Consistorial Court declared a marriage between a Presbyterian and an Episcopalian

Author's grandmother, c.*1930.*

celebrated by a Presbyterian minister illegal. The following year, a man convicted of bigamy carried the matter to a higher court, on the grounds that his first marriage, between a Presbyterian and Episcopalian and performed by a Presbyterian minister, was illegal. The Queen's Bench found in his favour. So great was the subsequent controversy that the government passed an Act in 1844 declaring valid not only future mixed marriages performed by Presbyterian ministers, but any past marriages.

This disability was not removed until 1870 for mixed marriages performed by Roman Catholic priests. Marriages between Roman Catholics and celebrated by Roman Catholic priests, on the other hand, have always been regarded as valid. They might be celebrated privately or publicly, at any time or place, and in any form or manner the celebrating priest thought proper, without banns, licence, notice, residence or consent. Marriages were usually in the bride's parish, in late afternoon or evening, many just before Christmas or between the Epiphany (6 January) and Shrove Tuesday, for sex was forbidden during Lent. The donations made at weddings were often the priests' main income. According to Dr John Forbes, who toured Ireland in the early 1850s:

> *The ordinary fee for marriage, even for the poor, is a guinea, sometimes 30s., and it is generally rigidly exacted ... Besides the regular fee, it is customary to make a collection at the house where the ceremony is performed, all the guests, often numerous, contributing more or less, according to their means, from 1s. to 5s or 10s. ... It is to be remarked that, in Ireland, the ceremony of marriage is almost always performed in private houses, and by licence; banns being very rarely published in chapel.*

For the Irish upper classes, marriage and property considerations were firmly intertwined. Until the mid-nineteenth century arranged marriages were the norm. As Lady Clonbrony put it in Maria Edgeworth's novel *The Absentee*: 'How could any body [not] out of Bedlam prefer to a good house, a decent equipage and a proper establishment what is called love in a cottage?' The normal marriage settlement consisted of a dowry or down payment by the bride's family to be matched by a settlement by the husband's family to pay her an allowance and provided for a jointure or pension for life if she should survive her husband.

Most Irish landed families married among themselves; in the case of the lesser gentry it was usually in the same or an adjoining county, which sometimes resulted in a satisfactory enlarging of estates and a jump in rank. Some of the lesser gentry were prepared to take the risk of abducting a suitable bride in order to improve their social position. In the south of Ireland there was a reported abduction club, with spies and emissaries in every country house to report on likely victims. According to J E Walsh, in his *Sketches of Ireland Sixty Years Age*, published in 1847, when a girl was selected

> *the members drew lots, but more generally tossed up for her, and immediate measures were taken to secure her for the fortunate man by all the rest ... When a girl fell to the lot of a member of the club, it was probable he never had known or spoken to her, but it was his care to meet her at a public ball, where he generally contrived to render himself agreeable, and in the bustle and confusion of breaking up to put her into a chaise, or on horseback, with or without her consent.*

Marriage as an institution was nevertheless highly valued in Irish society. In the 1840s Mr and Mrs Hall noted on a visit to Kerry that: 'second marriages are very rare amongst the peasantry, and comparatively so among the higher classes. This affords strong proof of the depth of their attachment, and they do not hold it to be strictly right for either men or women to marry again'. Some of the customs surrounding marriage surprised English visitors. Mr and Mrs Hall were amazed by a local custom for choosing a bride:

> *A few days before our arrival, an occurrence took place which we understand is by no means uncommon – a race for a wife. A young man, a carpenter, named Linchigan, applied to the father of a girl named Corrigan, for his daughter in marriage. A rival, called Lavelle, asked for her also, on the plea that as he was richer, 'he wouldn't ask so much with her'. Whereupon, the factions 'of the swains' were about to join issue and fight; when a peacemaker suggested that 'the boys should run for her'. The race was run accordingly, a distance of some miles up and down a mountain; Linchigan won, and wedded the maiden.*

The usual age for the marriage of women seems to have been between 15 and 20, and a young man would marry from the age of 20 upwards. Early marriage was blamed by contemporary writers for the poverty of the cotter and labouring classes in Ireland. Lieutenant J Greatorex, in his memoir for Aghalurcher in County Fermanagh written in the 1830s, declared:

> *It is customary as soon as the children of a family grow up for them to marry, usually at an early age, and begin the work on their own account, building mud huts wherever a few acres of land are to be obtained, and struggling through life in poverty and wretchedness, but apparently contented and cheerful.*

According to the *First Report from His Majesty's Commissioners for Inquiring into the Conditions of the Poorer Classes in Ireland*, 1835, early marriage was a strategy for survival among the poor. One witness told the inquiry:

> *I think early marriages are most useful here; a man looks forward to being supported in age by his family ... if a man marry at the age of 35, he will be broken down and unable to work before his children can be grown enough to support him ... but when a man marry young, his children will be able to support him before he is beyond his labour.*

The practice of early marriage in Ireland meant a great many children and, from the end of the seventeenth century, a rapid rise in the population. According to the census commissioners the number of births was around 265,000 per year between 1831 and 1841. For most poor women, childbirth took place at home with the help of family and neighbours unless relieved by some local charitable institution. Lying-in hospitals were found in many towns, financed by local subscription, with the aim of providing medical aid and attendance during their period of confinement. The records of the Belfast Lying-in Hospital, opened in 1790s, show that there was a separate ward for unmarried women, who were only admitted if they were first offenders. Weekly visitors were appointed from among the ladies of the committee. In the report book one of them states: 'I have endeavoured to make the midwife sensible that it is her duty to prevent the patients from spitting on the walls at the head of their beds.'

Geordie Ryan (the uncle of the author's grandmother), Canada Regiment.

It is clear from the Poor Law Inquiry of the 1830s that for single women having children could plunge them into destitution. In the Union of Templemichael and Ballymacormic, the commissioners were told:

> *Women who have illegitimate children are, according to two witnesses [Mr Carbery, general merchant – Revd Mr O'Donoghue, Roman Catholic clergyman], constantly compelled to resort to begging ... The difficulty of supporting herself and the child leads rather to begging than prostitution. The refusal of the reputed father to maintain the child produces in most cases ill feeling between the parties, and sometimes is the cause of violence.*

Another witness from the parish of Castlepollard, Co. Westmeath, declared 'Girls who have had illegitimate children are looked on with great contempt both by men and women, and are seldom married, nor would a farmer give his daughter to a bastard except he was much richer.'

Illegitimate children abandoned by their parents were largely placed on the parish. The cost of their maintenance came from a cess, a tax imposed on householders in the parish to meet parochial expenses. Some churchwardens went so far as to have foundling children removed from their parish under cover of darkness and left in a neighbouring parish. In 1722 the Archbishop of Dublin, Dr King, wrote to his clergy referring to this practice of 'dropping' children. He denounced it as a 'wicked practice' and he urged his ministers and their churchwardens to avoid the guilt of such acts since many children were subsequently killed.

It is hardly surprising, given the fight for survival many in Ireland faced throughout their lives, that travel writers during the eighteenth and nineteenth century commented that the Irish placed great emphasis on the manner of their send-off. Mr and Mrs Hall who visited Ireland in 1840 noted:

> *The most anxious thoughts of the Irish peasant all through his life are concerned with his death, and he will endure the extreme of poverty in order that he may scrape together the means of obtaining a 'fine wake' and a 'decent funeral'. He will, indeed, hoard for this purpose, although he will economise for no other, and it is by no means rare to find among a family clothed with rags and living in entire wretchedness, a few untouched garments laid aside for the*

day of burial. Only a month ago we gave a poor woman, an inmate of our parish workhouse, a few shillings. On asking her soon afterwards what she had done with the money, she said she had purchased a fine calico under-garment to be kept for her shroud so that she might be buried decently.

One custom that intrigued visitors to Ireland was that of 'waking' the dead. John Wesley was shocked by the 'Irish howl' which followed his speech at a burial service in Ireland in 1750. This was the 'dismal inarticulate yell' of four mourning women who were hired to stand by the grave and raise the lament. 'But I saw not one that shed a tear', he commented, 'for that, it seems, was not in their bargain'. According to Mr and Mrs Hall a century later:

The ceremonies differ somewhat in various districts, but only in a few minor and unimportant particulars. The body, decently laid out on a table or bed, covered with white linen, and not unfrequently adorned with black ribbons, if an adult, white, if the party be unmarried; and flowers, if a child. Close by it, or upon it, are plates of tobacco and snuff; around it are lighted candles. Usually a quantity of salt is laid upon it also. The women of the household range themselves at either side, and the keen (caoine) at once commences. They rise with one accord and, moving their bodies with a slow motion to and fro, their arms apart, they continue to keep up a heart-rending cry. During pauses of the women's wailing, the men, seated in groups by the fire, or in the corners of the room, are indulging in jokes, stories and bantering with each other – the subject of their conversation 'prices and politics, priests and parsons'.

For those who spent their life serving others, the pecking order in the next life mattered a great deal. It was commonly held that the last person to be interned in a graveyard had to serve the others until relieved of that duty by a fresh arrival. Mr and Mrs Hall noted:

If two funerals meet at the same churchyard, a contest immediately takes place to discover which will enter first, and happily, if decrying each other at a distance, it is only a contest of speed, for it is often a contest of strength, terminating in bloodshed and sometimes in death. This arises from the belief that the last person buried in a churchyard is employed in bringing water to his fellow tenants of the 'narrow house' until he is relieved in turn by the arrival of a newcomer.

Despite the high mortality rates in Ireland for much of the eighteenth and nineteenth centuries, according to the available figures, the population of Ireland rose dramatically. The estimates for the late seventeenth century put the population at around 1.5 million, and this had risen to 6,801,827 by 1821, the year of the first complete census for the country. By 1841, the last census before the Great Famine, the population had risen to 8,175,124. During the terrible years between the mid-1840s and the early 1850s more than 1 million died and another million emigrated. Although the worst of the blight was over by 1850 the population continued to fall throughout the remainder of the century, a combination of emigration, delayed marriages and celibacy. By 1900 it had fallen to approximately half of its pre-level, a decline that did not finally reverse until the 1960s, making Ireland unique in Europe.

Chapter 2

IRISH COUNTY LIFE

By the middle of the nineteenth century more than three-quarters of the Irish population lived in rural areas working in agriculture or in agricultural-related occupations. The Irish countryside was made up of great estates where, by the 1870s, more than half the land was owned by less than 1,000 major landlords, many of them related by blood or marriage. Many proprietors, like the Dukes of Devonshire, lived most of the year in England, returning occasionally to their Irish estates which were partly sub-let to lesser landlords and partly managed in their absence by agents or middlemen. At the other end of the social scale were the poor labourers walking the roads in search of work. In their absence their families frequently lived by begging, especially during the 'hungry months' or 'meal months' of June and July after the year's stock of potatoes had been used up and before the new ones became available.

The major landowners who managed great estates were often distributed through two or three counties; the Marquis of Downshire had 115,000 acres in Antrim, Down, Kildare, King's County and Wicklow; Lord Landsdowne owned 120,000 acres in Counties Dublin, Kerry, Limerick, Meath and Queen's; and the Marquis of Conyngham owned more than 156,000 acres in Clare, Donegal and Meath. Visitors to Ireland were struck by the great mansion houses like Powerscourt, Castletown and Castle Coole. Traditionally referred to as 'big houses' by the local community, in most cases the size of the landed estate dictated the size

An Irish cabin in Derrynane Beg. Pictorial Times *(1846).*

of the big house. Chevalier de la Tocnaye, a Frenchman who travelled through Ireland in the 1790s, was impressed by Lord Belmore's classical house, Castle Coole, in County Fermanagh.

> *Lord Belmore has just built in this neighbourhood, a superb palace, the masonry alone of the building costing him £80,000 sterling. The colonnade of the front elevation is of an architecture too fine, perhaps, for an individual and for a country house. The interior is full of rare marbles, and the walls of several rooms are covered with rare stucco work produced at great cost, and by workers brought from Italy.*

Many of the major landowners played a crucial role in the economic development of the county, particularly in the areas of agriculture, linen production and the establishment of market towns. The local gentry were the source from which magistrates were recruited, members of parliament were chosen and they dominated county administration until 1898. Many landlords also took an interest in education. Mr and Mrs Hall commented:

> *The principal proprietor of Tanderagee is Lord Manderville, who, with his neighbours, Lords Farnham and Roden, Colonel Blacker and*

the Marquis of Downshire, have contributed largely to the present cheering condition of the county of Armagh. Lord Manderville has established no fewer than sixteen district schools on his estate in this neighbourhood, for the support of which he devotes £1000 per annum, out of an income which is by no means large.

Right up until the First World War, and in some cases beyond that period, servants were an integral part of big house life in Ireland. They ensured a luxurious and leisured lifestyle for landlords by taking care of everything from caring for the richly furnished interiors of houses to cultivating extensive and elaborate gardens. The larger the house, the larger the number of servants required to cope with the number of tasks involved. In 1911, the Marquis of Conyngham, for example, employed a private nurse, a governess, two lady's maids, a butler, cook, housekeeper, valet, two footmen, a hall boy, as well as scullery, kitchen, parlour, dairy and house maids at Slane. Recruitment of staff was usually through personal recommendations, particularly at the higher levels of housekeeper, governess and cook. Local Irish women found most opportunities for employment at the lower levels as maids in the house, kitchen, nursery or dairy. According to the 1871 census, domestic service accounted for almost 15 per cent of the female workforce. Certain families provided servants over several generations in the same house.

Servant life was not an easy one. Staff could be dismissed for unsatisfactory service. Mr and Mrs Hall condemned the treatment of Irish servants. 'They are insufficiently remunerated; little care is bestowed upon their wants; they are seldom properly fed and lodged ...' An 'odious and evil custom' which they took objection to was the mode of paying servants what was called 'breakfast money', which was a small allowance allotted to them by their employees for food and the other necessities of life.

The almost inevitable consequence is that of the weekly allowance they contrive to save a considerable portion, or nearly the whole, usually with a view to devoting the quarter's wages untouched to the necessities of their more miserable families 'at home' ... thus they are subjected to severe privations in the midst of plenty, if they scrupulously abstain from taking that which, by this rule, is not to belong to them.

Farm labourers. Attributed to Augusta Colborn, c.*1857*.

Farmwork, the cultivation of extensive and often elaborate gardens and the preservation of game provided a good deal of employment on demesnes as at Powerscourt, where up to fifty men were employed at high season. Demesne employees included gardeners, grooms, coachmen, agricultural labourers, herds, shepherds, gamekeepers, yardmen, blacksmiths, foresters, carpenters, masons and plasterers. It was the job of the steward to supervise the overall activities of demesne employees who were often members of the same family and worked as retainers for generations.

Tenant farmers and their families accounted for half the rural population, numbering about 500,000 in the 1860s. They leased their land from the landlords and worked full-time on the land, cultivating with their immediate family and hired labourers. As a group they were more varied than the landlords, their holdings ranging from a few acres to large graziers such as Edward Delany of Woodtown who held 500 acres in Co. Meath. Usually referred to locally as 'respectable' when commentators wished to distinguish between them and the average tenant who held their land from year to year, one observer in the 1840s defined them as having 'very comfortable and independent circumstances ... they settle their sons well and give large portions [dowries] to their daughters on their marriage'.

Many of these farmers were also landlords to the smallholders and cotters, subletting land which they rented on long leases from the landowner. Condemned by many contemporaries as landjobbers, lease speculators or, more commonly, middlemen, many had benefited under the long leases and low rents offered by landlords in the depressed late seventeenth century and the rapid rise in land rents after 1750 by raising their own tenants' rents in line with changing market conditions. One of their fiercest critics, Arthur Young, condemned them in the 1770s: 'Living upon the spot, surrounded by their little under-tenants, they prove the most oppressive species of tyrant that ever lent assistance to the destruction of a country.' The importance of middlemen declined during the nineteenth century as landlords increasingly let directly to occupying tenants. The Great Famine completed this process by bankrupting those middlemen responsible for paying the poor rate on behalf of their own numerous impoverished smallholders.

Most tenants had a yearly tenancy and could be evicted with only six months' notice to quit; rents could be increased annually and evicted tenants had no right to compensation for improvements. The Ulster Custom in the north left the tenants in a much better position than those in the other provinces. It was a practice or usage by which a tenant paying rent to his landlord should not be evicted without being paid by the incoming tenant, or by the landlord, the full marketable price of his interest in the farm, this interest being the value of his own improvements and those inherited from his ancestors. This custom ensured that the landlord could not raise the rent as the tenant effected improvements in his holding. The tenant benefited from his own efforts, and this encouraged him to be hard-working and law-abiding. Englishman John Gough, who visited Ireland in 1813–14, noted the difference in attitude of tenants in the North: 'How very different is the situation of the common people in Ulster province, though living under the same government, and subject to the very same laws. There, the poorest man, looking upon himself as a man, would not tamely submit to unmerited insult from anyone.'

Further down the social scale were the cotter tenants who worked for a landlord and lived in cottages provided by him on his estate. They also

Irish gleaner. Illustrated London News *(1852).*

rented small portions of land upon which to grow potatoes, oats and possibly some flax. They held the ground on a year-to-year basis and their rent was often paid in labour. In the 1770s Arthur Young left a vivid description of the cotter class:

> *If there are cabins on a farm they are the residence of the cotters. If there are none the farmer marks out the potato gardens, and the labourers, who apply to him on his hiring the land, raise their own cabins on such spots; in some places the farmer builds, in others he only assists them with the roof, etc. A verbal compact is then made, that the new cotter shall have his potato garden at such a rent, and one or two cows kept him at the price of the neighbourhood, he finding the cows. He then works with the farmer at the rate of the place, usually 6½ a day, a tally being kept (half by each party), and a notch cut for every day's labour; at the end of six months, or a year, they reckon, and the balance is paid. The cotter works for himself as his potatoes require.*

The cotter class, heavily dependent upon the potato as they were, almost completely disappeared after the Great Famine.

Potato dinner. Pictorial Times *(1846).*

The largest group found in the countryside, and at the bottom of the social scale, was agricultural labourers. Many labourers were casually employed and they could be thrown out of their cottages with only a few weeks' notice. They often moved from place to place in search of work. Although ostensibly employed on one of the great estates they generally worked for one of the tenants and therefore are not mentioned in the great estate collections; nor can they be picked up in the electoral registers because they did not have the vote until 1885. The poor labourer walking the roads in search of work was a common sight until the late nineteenth century. The first of these migrants made their appearance in the spring, when the ground was being broken up for tillage. At the end of the season he took his pay and set off again to his own place, to dig potatoes or save his own little crop. By the end of the nineteenth century the migrant workers had all but disappeared. Machines were being developed to carry out various farm operations and they greatly reduced the need for outside labour. But the poor man continued to offer his labour further afield. From Donegal to Mayo they went to Scotland, for seasonal work on the potato crops; from further south they went to the cities in search of building work, and often never came back.

Thurles Market. Illustrated London News *(1848)*.

In the countryside, women played an important role in bringing in extra money to the household. Harriet Martineau wrote in 1852:

> *we observe women working almost everywhere. In the flax-fields there are more women than men pulling and steeping. In the potato-fields it is often the women who are saving the remnant of the crop. In the harvest-fields there are as many women as men reaping and binding. In the bog, it is the women who, at half wages, set up, and turn, and help to stack the peat – not only for household use, but for sale, and in the service of the Irish Peat Company.*

There was a dramatic change in the range of agricultural work available to women by the end of the nineteenth century. Changing land-usage patterns, the shift from tillage to dairying, increased stock rearing which was less labour intensive, growing levels of mechanization and the coming of the creameries, which removed butter-making from the home, all took their toll on women's agricultural opportunities.

Visitors to the Irish countryside were struck by the level of poverty. In 1841, 40 per cent of the houses in Ireland were one-room mud cabins. Furniture in these cabins usually consisted of a bed of straw, a crude table and stool and a few cooking utensils. Labourer and cotter shared a potato diet. Mr and Mrs Hall found that

> *The peasant usually has three meals – one at eight in the morning, at noon, and at seven or eight in the evening when his work is done. The potatoes are boiled in an iron pot and strained in the basket from which they are thrown upon the table – seldom without a cloth – and around which the family sit on stools and bosses (the boss is a low seat made of straw). The usual drink is buttermilk when it can be had, and it goes around in a small piggin, a sort of miniature English pail.*

Only at Christmas was there a chance of meat. The small farmer's diet might also include milk, oatmeal and wheaten bread: their main luxuries were tobacco and drink.

Dress varied even within the various elements of rural society. The better-off farmer wore knee britches, waistcoat, shirt and cravat, tailcoat and sturdy boots. His wife wore a cloak which covered a bodice, 'midi'-skirt and shift. The lower grades had generally the same cut of clothes, but they were more ragged and patched. Few of the labourers had overcoats and the women and children generally went barefoot. Among the very poor clothing was little better than rags. Dr John Forbes condemned men in the 1850s for their

> *abominable habit, so long prevalent among the poor in Ireland, of wearing the cast-off clothes of others. This habit, originating, no doubt, in poverty, has, I think, been carried much further than was absolutely necessary, merely because it had become a habit. I think it must be beginning to wear out, as I observe that a fair proportion of the boys and young men show themselves, as least on Sundays, in jackets and short coats, evidently originals.... Nothing could convey to a stranger a stronger impression of wretchedness and untidiness, than this vicarious costume of the Irish, disfiguring at once to the person of the wearers, and calling forth in the mind of the observer the most disagreeable associations. Even when not in holes, as they too often are, those long-tailed coats almost touching the ground, and those shapeless breeches with their gaping knee-bands sagging below the calf of the leg, are the very emblems and ensigns of beggary and degradation.*

For the tenant farmer two issues were paramount – tithe and rents. The tithe system, which nominally earmarked one-tenth of the produce of the land for the maintenance of the established clergy, was introduced in Ireland during the reign of Henry II although they were not paid outside the area around Dublin until the sixteenth century. Originally the tithes were payable in kind such as the tenth cow or sheep etc. The tithe, paid half-yearly in November and May, was difficult to collect and uneven in its levy. Tithe was generally collected not by the incumbent clergyman but by a tithe-farmer or tithe-proctor acting on his behalf. The clergyman received a fixed sum and the excess was retained by the proctor who had therefore strong motivation to exact every last penny. According to the *Statistical Account for County Clare*, published in 1808,

> *The rates of tithe vary according to the disposition of the clergyman or his tithe-proctor, and are a tolerable barometer of the love or dislike of his parishioners; where they are higher than customary,*

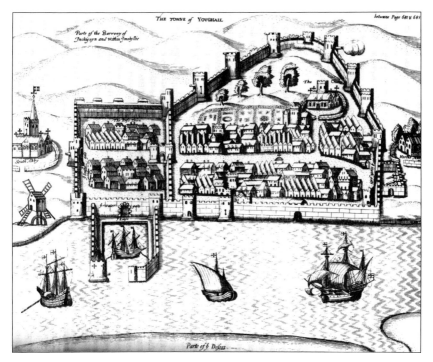

Youghal from Pacata Hibernia, Ireland Appeased and Reduced *(1633).*

> *you may be certain of finding a turbulent divine, who will have his rights, regardless whether he is liked or disliked, or, if he is a non-resident, his proctor is of the same way of thinking. If, on the contrary, they are moderately exacted, the love and respect of his neighbours follow of course.*

Inevitably the proctor was unpopular in local communities. As more peasants crowded the land, resistance to the payment of tithe increased. The Tithe Applotment Act of 1823, which specified that the tithe should now be paid in cash, sought to address the unpopularity of paying in kind but the charge remained unpopular. Eventually the government gave way to popular pressure and introduced the Tithe Rent Charge Act in 1838 which reduced by 25 per cent the tithe payment and transferred it from the tenant to the landowner. The tithe rent charge was lost to the church on disestablishment (1 January 1871) but continued to be paid by occupiers

A Galway election scene depicted in Lever's Charles O'Malley *(1841).*

to a body called the Commissioners of Church Temporalities and, on the dissolution of that body in 1881, to the Irish Land Commission.

Rents were usually paid half-yearly: the county rents were due on 1 May and 1 November while town leases were often due on 25 March (old New Year's Day, known as Lady Day or the Annunciation of the Blessed Virgin Mary) and 29 September (Michaelmas). Tenants, cotters and agricultural labourers who had difficulty paying their rents faced the constant threat of eviction. Evictions are popularly associated with the

Great Famine, but they took place in large numbers throughout the nineteenth century and indeed before that; the later half of the eighteenth century is peppered with accounts of tenants being ejected from their homes.

Landowners were greatly assisted by the fact that the process of eviction before the Land Act of 1879 was simple and quick. It usually took the form of threats of eviction before notices to quit were served on the tenants. The forcible removal of the tenant by the subsheriff was carried out, assisted if necessary by the constabulary. This process could take place only with the approval of a court. If the court decided in the landlord's favour, he was given an ejectment decree, which was an order to the sheriff to give the landlord possession of the holding. The decree had to be executed within a certain period – it could not he held indefinitely as a threat to the tenant. It had to be executed on a week-day between 9 am and 3 pm; it could not, after 1848, be executed on Christmas Day or Good Friday. The landlord or his agent had to inform the relieving officer at least forty-eight hours before the eviction took place; failure to do so could lead to a fine of £20. The amount of force that could be used was strictly regulated. It was, for example, a mis-demeanour to unroof a house while it was still occupied. A tenant evicted for non-payment had six months in which to redeem his holding by paying arrears and costs.

Many landowners cared little for the niceties of the law, and their willingness to use force to evict tenants became increasingly marked during the Great Famine. The system of poor relief introduced into Ireland in 1838 was financed out of local rates and, as the workhouses began to fill up with the sick and destitute, the chief costs fell upon the landlords, many of whom were already burdened with debt. Their income was badly affected by the non-payment of rents and they were forced to sell their estates often heavily mortgaged. During the 1850s more than five million acres, almost a quarter of the land in Ireland, passed into the hands of new landlords, many of whom were wealthy speculators. The more progressive of these saw eviction as a necessary first step to improving land management on their estates.

William Gladstone's Land Act of 1870 gave the so-called 'Ulster Custom' a legal backing. The tenant had the right to sell his interest in his holding and to obtain the appropriate compensation for any improvements he had made; and he would be less likely to suffer eviction since if he were evicted he would be entitled to a reasonable degree of compensation. The Act was greeted with disappointment by many tenants. Most of them still had no security of tenure and their rents could still be raised at will. The machinery for operating the Act also remained inadequate. In a dispute between the landlord and tenant, the burden of proof was put upon the tenant who had to take his case before a county court judge. This was likely to be a costly procedure while compensation payments for improvements and disturbance tended to be low. Nevertheless, it was a major step forward, giving Irish tenants rights that no British government would have considered giving to English farmers.

Rural violence was nevertheless on the increase, with the number of burnings, shootings and cattle-maimings rising to 2,590 by 1880. Among the landlords killed was Lord Mountmorris, dispatched in his strong-hold in Co. Galway. On 2 April 1878, William Clements, 3rd Lord Leitrim, who owned property amounting to 94,535 acres, including an estate of 54,352 acres in North Donegal, was murdered. His arrogance and brutality had become a byword which alienated him even from members of his own class. He had removed all the tenants of Rawros to build his castle at Manorvaughan and those at Cratlagh to plant a vista of trees; he had a chapel pulled down with the aid of crowbar men and forced a farmer keeping goats against the rules to kill them on the spot before his eyes.

In attempt to address the land issue, Gladstone introduced a Bill in 1881 to bring about a radical reform of the Irish land system. Its leading feature was a Land Commission to adjudicate rents, and therefore to establish the principle of dual ownership of land, by both owners and tenants, into the law. The new Act also guaranteed the tenant fixity of tenure provided he paid the rent and gave him the right to sell his holding, together with any improvements he had made to it, to an incoming tenant. Although it did not go far enough for many, it worked well. The rents fixed by the land courts were reasonable and the return of better potato harvests meant that the crisis on the land was temporarily easing. On the other hand, landlords experienced reductions in rent which averaged out at around 20 per cent. As one contemporary observer noted, there was an unpleasant irony to this: 'The landlords who have suffered least have probably been those who simplified their properties by wholesale evictions.'

A series of Land Acts followed, culminating in the 1903 Act, popularly known as the Wyndham Act, which offered the landlords a 12 per cent bonus in addition to the agreed price if they agreed to sell out their entire estate. The Act also introduced the principle of sale of the whole estate, with tenants agreeing to common terms, rather than the piecemeal sale of holdings. Provision was also made for the purchase of estates by the Land Commission and the resale of untenanted lands to uneconomic holders or evicted tenants. The Act was popular with tenants because it guaranteed annual repayments lower than existing rents.

Therefore by the beginning of the twentieth century, government legislation had brought about in Ireland a complete revolution in land ownership. Within a generation the position of the landlords in Ireland had

Winnowing corn farmer, Mourne Mountains, c.1915. Green Collection, Ulster Museum.

been altered as the land passed into the hands of the former tenants. 'The Act undid the confiscations of James I, Cromwell, and William III', as Nationalist MP Tim Healy a supporter of the Wyndham Act remarked. Between 1870 and 1933 tenants in what is now the Republic of Ireland, bought out 450,000 holdings, a total of 15 million acres out of 17 million. The land question had, at last, been removed from Irish politics.

Chapter 3

LIFE IN THE TOWNS AND CITIES

Until its overthrow in the seventeenth century, Gaelic Ireland was basically a rural society with few urban settlements. Although the more important monastic settlements at Armagh, Clonard and Bangor developed large populations, it was not the arrival of the Vikings that a number of coastal trading towns developed in the ninth century. Among these are the modern ports: Dublin, Cork, Waterford, Wexford and Limerick. Later towns, such as Galway, Dungannon and Carrickfergus, were established by the Anglo-Normans. Ireland remained overwhelmingly rural until the late nineteenth century. Although the 1841 census states that one-fifth of the population of Ireland were town-dwellers; this is misleading as this includes any settlement exceeding twenty houses. Only five centres, Dublin, Cork, Belfast, Limerick and Waterford, had more than 20,000 inhabitants.

Between the Norman and Tudor periods, although English settlers mingled with the Irish in other parts of the country, and adopted their manners and customs, the towns were kept apart. Surrounded by their walls and heavily garrisoned, they defied the natives and were centres of English influence and power. In return for their support the English kings bestowed upon them so many privileges that they became almost independent. In medieval times, while the invaders with their families and servants resided within the walled town, the Irish often lived outside the gates, supplying the garrison with provisions or giving their services as workmen or labourers. This seems to have been the origin of the 'English' and 'Irish' quarters in Irish towns which were still to be found in the eighteenth century.

In Queen Elizabeth's reign there were at least forty-three walled cities and towns in Ireland, many of which were not only independent but rich, for they had built up an extensive trade during the Middle Ages with the Continent, and especially with Spain. With the Tudor conquest of Ireland, these cities and towns lost their importance and independence and by the beginning of the eighteenth century the walls, towers, castles and fortified houses of the Irish towns had for the most part disappeared or fallen into decay, as the result partly of continuous warfare and partly of the economic depression which accompanied it.

As a result, by the sixteenth century towns were most numerous in the south and east of Ireland, in the areas most effectively controlled by the Crown. All this was to change dramatically in the seventeenth century thanks to the Plantation of Ulster. The establishment of towns was regarded as an essential element in the Plantation scheme. Towns

College Street, Dublin, 1828.

were seen as a strong point where colonists could be mustered for defence; as providing centres for civil administration and justice; and as stimulating economic growth, in the development of commercial agriculture and the production and sale of manufactured goods.

The locations of twenty-five corporate towns were chosen by the planners of the Ulster Plantation for their strategic value. Some were based on forts erected during the campaigns of the previous decade, such as Charlemont and Mount Norris in Co. Armagh; others were on the sites of native strongholds like Dungannon, or monasteries such as Derry. However, it was economic potential rather than military strategy which determined their growth. The Plantation towns were planned settlements, strictly regular in the layout of streets and building, and very different to the haphazard development of medieval towns like Kilkenny or Galway. The towns that had grown the most by the end of the seventeenth century were those best located to stimulate trade based on the development of commercial agriculture. The most important towns, such as Derry, Strabane, Limavady or Coleraine, were situated in fertile valleys; and these were also the areas most densely settled by British colonists. By the end of the century there were more than a hundred settlements in Ulster which might properly be called towns.

The most backward towns in Ireland were generally in the interior, where there were no flourishing industries to promote their growth. They were mere centres of exchange, where farmers and graziers came to dispose of their produce and to buy such commodities as they did not manufacture themselves. They also became important administrative centres. In a market town at the centre of a large agricultural area, trade with the surrounding countryside was the main business of life, and the main streets to this day are full of shops, banks and insurance offices. By the beginning of the Victorian era, many also included a bank and within twenty years a railway station which carried agricultural produced to the major ports.

Most towns had regular fairs; the fair green survives as a reminder of the great social and commercial importance of these public gatherings. According to the *Statistical Survey of Armagh*, published in 1804:

> *The fairs and markets are, in general, well attended by retailers of hats, stockings, shoes, cloth, and wool, from other counties; and also*

Market women at the Old Booths, Galway. Illustrated London News *(1879).*

by pedlars, whose stock consists of articles of apparel, principally of women's wear, and hard-ware. These itinerant dealers are always travelling from one market town to another; some of them have no fixed residence.

Author William Makepeace Thackeray described a fair he encountered at Naas in the 1840s:

the town, as we drove into it, was thronged with frieze-coats, the market-place bright with a great number of apple-stalls, and the street filled with carts and vans of numerous small tradesmen, vending cheeses, or cheap crockeries, or ready-made clothes and such goods. A clothier, with a great crowd round him, had arrayed himself in a staring [sic] new waistcoat of his stock, and was turning slowly round to exhibit the garment, spouting all the while to his audience, and informing them that he could fit out any person, in one minute, 'in a complete new suit from head to fut.' There seemed to be a crowd of gossips at every shop-door, and, of course, a number of gentlemen waiting at the inn-steps, criticising the cars and carriages as they drove up.

Many towns were small and almost invariably shabby, their approaches lined with poor hovels, their streets interspersed with ruins. Until the mid-nineteenth century often a military barracks was the only substantial building in the town. Shortly after the Union it was estimated that there were from 30,000 to 50,000 regular troops stationed in Ireland, besides 21,000 militiamen and numerous bodies of yeomanry, so it is not surprising to find that military barracks were often the finest and most magnificent buildings in the Irish towns of the period. The fact that town rents were often higher in Ireland than in England was popularly ascribed to the temporary residence of the military, and this probably helped to make them unpopular with the inhabitants, especially as their behaviour was often far from orderly. The soldiers were, however, often the chief support of the local tradesmen, the officers generally dining at taverns, while the common soldiers bought meat and other provisions in the shops.

During the nineteenth century Dublin remained the biggest city in Ireland. Unlike Belfast, its rival in the north, it was not heavily industrialized. Dublin remained an administrative, military and cultural capital, noted for its public buildings. Founded by the Vikings, by the medieval period the town consisted of Norse, English and Irish traders who exported woollens, pelts and combs. Dublin Castle, Christ Church Cathedral and St Patrick's Cathedral survive from this period and bear testimony to the growing city's importance.

Dublin was at its grandest at the end of the eighteenth century with its wealthier citizens enjoying a leisured lifestyle in the new housing areas to the east of the old city. The south-east, containing St Stephen's Green, Merrion Square and Fitzwilliam Square, was dominated by the nobility, gentry and professions. Amongst the highest class of residence, Arthur Young found in the late eighteenth century that

> *all there is gaiety, pleasure, luxury, and extravagance. The town life at Dublin is formed on the model of that of London. Every night in the winter there is a ball or a party where the polite circle meet, not to enjoy but to sweat each other: a crowd crammed into twenty feet square gives a zest to the agreements of small talk and whist.*

The Act of Union, 1800, and the abolition of the Irish Parliament, resulted in the upper levels of society leaving for London. Dublin's faded

Dublin Castle in the 1840s. From a photograph by W H Fox-Talbot.

St Stephen's Green with statue of George II. From aquatint by James Maiton.

grandeur lingered on, however, and impressed visitors to the city throughout the nineteenth century. Thackeray's first impressions of Dublin was that the

> *entrance to the capital is very handsome. There is no bustle and throng of carriages, as in London; but you pass by numerous rows of neat houses, fronted with gardens and adorned with all sorts of gay-looking creepers. Pretty market-gardens, with trim beds of plants and shining glass-houses, give the suburbs a riante and cheerful look; and, passing under the arch of the railway, we are in the city itself. Hence you come upon several old-fashioned, well-built, airy, stately streets, and through Fitzwilliam Square, a noble place, the garden of which is full of flowers and foliage. The leaves are green, and not black as in similar places in London; the red brick houses tall and handsome.*

Henry D Inglis, who visited the Irish capital in 1834, was also struck by the grandeur of the city.

> *A stranger arriving in Dublin in Spring, as I did, will be struck, even less by the architectural beauty of the city, than by other kinds of splendour: I allude to the indulgences of luxury, and the apparent*

The Rotunda and Rutland Square. From a print by S F Brocas, c.1820.

proofs of wealth that are everywhere thrust upon the eye – the numerous private vehicles that fill the streets, and even blockade many of them; the magnificent shops for the sale of articles of luxury and taste, at the doors of which, in Grafton Street, I have counted upwards of twenty handsome enquipages; and in certain quarters of the city, the number of splendid houses, and 'legion' of liveried servants.

The other side of Dublin life also made an impression on Inglis as he stayed in house in Kildare Street which was exactly opposite to the Royal Dublin Society then exhibiting a cattle-show.

After the cattle had been fed, the half-eaten turnips became the prerequisite of the crowd of ragged boys and girls without. Many and fierce were the scrambles for these precious relics; and a half-gnawed turnip, once secured, was guarded with the most vigilant jealousy, and was lent for a mouthful to another longing tatter-demalion, as much apparently as an act of extraordinary favour, as if the root had been a pineapple.

As the gentry left the Irish capital for London, the inner city became increasingly associated with poverty and slums as the population grew from 182,000 in 1800 to 285,000 in 1851. The wealthy had vacated

Turf Market, Dublin. Illustrated London News *(1843).*

substantial townhouses in aristocratic distracts such as Gardiner Street and Summer Hill on the north side and these one-family homes were rapidly subdivided to accommodate at least one family per room. The Revd James Whitelaw, rector of St Catherine's Church in Thomas Street, carried out a census in 1798. He put the population of the city at 172,091. Of the Liberties, most of which lay south-west of the river, in the oldest part of the city, he wrote:

> *The streets are generally narrow; the houses crowded together; the rears or backyards of very small extent, and some without accommodation of any kind. Of these streets, a few are the residence of the upper class of shopkeepers or others engaged in trade; but a far greater proportion of them, with their numerous lanes and alleys, are occupied by working manufacturers, by petty shop-keepers, the labouring poor, and beggars, crowded together to a degree distressing to humanity ... As I was usually out at very early hours on the survey I have frequently surprised from ten to sixteen persons, of all ages and sexes, in a room not 15 feet square, stretched on a wad of filthy straw, swarming with vermin, and*

without any covering, save the wretched rags that constituted their wearing apparel. Under such circumstances it is not extraordinary that I should have frequently found from 30 to 40 individuals in a house . . .

Diseases such as cholera, typhus and smallpox were endemic. Once generated, disease spread from room to room and from floor to floor of the city's slums and was carried back to the houses of the rich by servants and employees. Inadequate sewerage systems, poor water supplies, slaughterhouses and obnoxious activities such as soap-making and lime-burning right in the midst of the crowded population all contributed to the situation. The overcrowding condition of many of Dublin's cemeteries was another evil for its citizens. The Revd James Whitelaw writes in 1798:

St Mary's parish contains 16,654 souls and its churchyard about 32,000 square feet; hence the proportion for each inhabitant is not 2 square feet, and it is a fact, which I have witnessed, that in order to make room for others, bodies in that cemetery have been taken up in an absolute state of putrefaction, to the great and very dangerous annoyance of the vicinity.

By the end of the nineteenth century the high mortality rate among the Dublin poor reached the outrageous figure of 33.6 per 1,000; the London average was 19.6. The high rate was due largely to tuberculosis, most of whose victims were aged around 25 years. Free disinfection was offered to the residents of any Dublin dwelling in which a person suffering from consumption had died, but in the majority of cases this offer was refused. One doctor complained 'they will attend wakes, sleep, dwell or visit, in places teeming with infection, without a moment's misgiving, but as soon as ever the officer has been brought to disinfect a house or room, they shun it as if he had brought the plague instead of banishing it'.

Progress was made by Dublin Corporation over the years. More than 2,000 people in the Liberties were rehoused in the 1890s. Sanitary officers vigorously pursued, fined and named those found guilty of trading in adulterated food, and flush toilets spread rapidly after 1880. The Corporation took steps to close down dangerous housing, remove refuse, control slaughter-houses and appoint health inspectors. The migration of Dublin's wealthier households to the suburbs held back the city's capacity to address public health and housing issues until the beginning of the twentieth century, and it was not until the 1940s that a much delayed public housing programme finally banished the slums. The city portrayed in Joyce's *Dubliners* was being outshone by the rapidly expanding Belfast and, as a result of home rule, was divided along religious lines, with most of the banking and commercial communities being Protestant and Unionist in sympathy. It would not be until the end of the twentieth century that a new self-confident Dublin would emerge, fuelled by a booming economy.

By the eighteenth century, Cork was by far the most important port outside Dublin. The town was established by the Vikings in the tenth century and by the twelfth had become an Anglo-Norman fortified city. Lying south of the great grazing counties, Cork became an important city during the eighteenth century, exporting large quantities of provisions to the Continent, to the English colonies in America and to the West Indies. The trade of Cork, with its population of about 80,000 inhabitants, had grown so great, indeed, by the end of the eighteenth century that it was

Chapel-Lane Skibbereen. Illustrated London News *(1847).*

known as the 'Bristol of Ireland'. Arthur Young described it as 'by much the most animated busy scene of shipping in all Ireland'. Cork merchants grew extremely rich and, as many of them lived at one time or another either in France, Spain, or Portugal in connection with their business, they had often a foreign air which was reflected in their dress and manners.

By the middle of the nineteenth century, Dr John Forbes found similar conditions of wealth and poverty to those in Dublin:

Like all large towns, and more especially the large towns of Ireland, Cork contains masses of hidden streets of the most squalid description, inhabited by a ragged and seemingly wretched population. In passing through such streets, however, it is but just to the inhabitants to state that we saw no riotous or indecorous behaviour, and were but rarely solicited for charity. In going along the better streets, on Sunday, we observed many wretched-looking women, most of them with ragged children on their laps or by their side, squatted in the recesses of the doors of the shut shops, obviously beggars, yet not begging, except with that speaking look of misery more emphatic than words. Even the children were as silent as their mothers.

Limerick, originally a Norse settlement, became the seat of the O'Briens of Thomond in the late twelfth century and was granted a charter by Prince John in 1197. With its 60,000 inhabitants in the eighteenth century, Limerick had recovered from the great siege which concluded the Williamite War. It carried on a good trade in corn and provisions, for, although the city was more than sixty miles form the sea, ships of 500 tons were able to sail up the Shannon and unloaded their cargoes at the quays. Walking through the district of Newtown Pery, in the 1840s William Makepeace Thackeray commented:

you are at first led to believe that you are arrived in a second Liverpool, so tall are the warehouses and broad the quays; so neat and trim a street of near a mile which stretches before you. But even this mile-long street does not, in a few minutes, appear to be so wealthy and prosperous as it shows at first glance; for of the

The stocks, Dromore, c.1915. WAG1193.

*population that throng the streets, two-fifths are barefooted women,
and two-fifths more ragged men: and the most part of the shops
which have a grand show with them appear, when looked into, to be
no better than they should be, being empty makeshift-looking places
with their best goods outside.*

Waterford too was established by the Vikings. Captured by the
Normans in 1170 over the next four centuries it became one of the most
prosperous places in Ireland. The medieval economy was based on shipbuilding and trade, with the export of wool and hides to Flanders and
elsewhere. The medieval walls were demolished in the seventeenth century
as the town expanded, and fine Georgian streets and buildings replaced
the narrow medieval fabric. By the end of the eighteenth century, lead
crystal had become a leading industry. But by the nineteenth century,
Waterford like many Irish towns and cities was in decline and its
population fell from almost 40,000 in 1800 to 23,000 in 1841. That same
year Mr and Mrs Hall were of the opinion that

*Although Waterford is a mercantile city and one with advantages
peculiarly eligible and accessible, there is a sad aspect of loneliness*

in its streets and a want of business along its quays, except on those days when the steam boats leave and the live stock assembles in huge droves to embark for the English market. The hotels, too, usually sure indications of prosperity or its opposite, have a deserted look, and it would hardly be an exaggeration to say that the grass springs up between the steps that lead to their doors.

Until the middle of the nineteenth century Belfast, the most industrialized of Ireland's cities, lay entirely within the Donegall estate in Co. Antrim. One of the few major towns anywhere in Britain or Ireland to be owned entirely by one family, German traveller J G Kohl was amazed to find: 'This vast mass of human beings, and all the houses they inhabit, live and stand one and all on the ground and soil of one proprietor, the Marquis of Donegall, to whom the entire town belongs, to whom every citizen pays tribute.' The Donegalls had inherited this great legacy from Sir Arthur Chichester who was granted the land during the Plantation, and were to play a major role in the development of the town. They provided the town with some of its finest public buildings including St Anne's Church, the Assembly Rooms and Exchange and donated the land for the Poor House and the White Linen Hall. For most of the eighteenth century the Chichesters had lived in England. George Augustus, second marquis of Donegall, was forced by mounting debts to retire to Belfast in 1802. In an effort to clear the estate of debts, leases were granted for ever at the existing rents in return for cash payments. The new leaseholders, as long as the rents were paid, were now free to do as they liked and all control by the Donegall family over the future development of the town was removed.

During the second half of the nineteenth century Belfast grew more rapidly than any other city in the British Isles. Its prosperity was founded on three major industries: textiles, engineering and shipbuilding. During the second half of the nineteenth century the population of Belfast rose from 90,000 to 350,000. Only by constantly redrawing the city's boundary could Dublin keep its coveted position as the largest city in Ireland. In 1888 Queen Victoria granted Belfast city status, and four years later another charter conferred on the Mayor the title of 'Lord Mayor'. This charter declared that Belfast was the capital of the province of Ulster and that in commercial and manufacturing it was the first town

Raphael Street Belfast, 1912. Welch Collection, Ulster Museum.

in Ireland. Mr and Mrs Hall were impressed by the industrial character of the city which set it apart from the others they had visited in Ireland.

> *It is something new to perceive rising above the houses numerous tall and thin chimneys which are indicative of industry, occupation, commerce and prosperity, with the volumes of smoke that issued from them giving unquestionable tokens of full employment, while its vicinity to the ocean removed at once all idea that the labour was unwholesome or the labourers unhealthy.*

They went on to declare that 'The clean and bustling appearance of Belfast is decidedly unnational. That it is in Ireland, but not of it, is a remark often on the lips of visitors from the south or west.'

In common with other industrial cities of the time, Belfast had its share of slum housing in which the poor were forced to live in the most desperate conditions. Periodic slumps in the textile or cotton industries left many unemployed and forced to depend on charity. Those in work were often on the breadline when hard seasons raised the price of food. With widespread destitution came diseases such as cholera and typhus. According to one account written in March 1801:

> *The town subscribes alone 200 guineas a month to one charity – the soup house – and yet our streets and the inhabitants of our lanes present scenes of vice and wretchedness unequalled in former times. A habitation which I visited yesterday, filled by four generations of females, two confined on their straw by sickness, without a remnant of linen; a chair, stool or board to sit on, the spinning wheel at the pawnbrokers and all they once possessed, for once they were decent.*

Court scene. D H Hogg, Linen Hall Library.

The Medical Officer of Health in Belfast wrote in 1909 that 'consumption was most prevalent among the poor, owing largely to the unfavourable conditions under which necessity compels them to live – such as dark, ill-ventilated houses and insanitary habits, together with insufficient food and clothing'.

The Great Famine which devastated such much of the Ulster country-side only contributed to the rapid expansion of Belfast as people fled to the town in hope of work or charity. As Belfast's population grew, clashes between the different religious groups became an increasing feature of life in the town. Sectarian rivalry manifested itself in waves of rioting, beginning with a clash on 12 July 1813 and continuing throughout the nineteenth and twentieth centuries. Polling day battles in 1832, 1835 and 1841 had become by 1857 serious rioting that lasted for days or weeks. Various constitutional crises during the nineteenth century only exacerbated sectarianism within Belfast. Daniel O'Connell's campaign for Catholic Emancipation during the 1820s and his Repeal Movement of the 1840s held little appeal for Belfast Protestants. In 1844, a German traveller to Ireland, J G Kohl, recorded that O'Connell tended to avoid the town of Belfast during his tours of Ireland. Kohl was told of one particular incident during his visit to Belfast:

> *I was told at Belfast that the great musician Liszt had the misfortune to be taken for O'Connell in the neighbourhood of that city, and was very near undergoing something extremely disagreeable that was intended for the agitator. As Liszt approached from Newry, in a handsome chaise drawn by four horses, and it was rumoured that the carriage contained a celebrated man, some of the Presbyterian rabble imagined it was O'Connell. They stopped the carriage, cut the traces, and compelled the eminent pianist to dismount, in order that they might wreak their anger against him in Irish fashion. They merely wished to duck him in a neighbouring pond, and then to advise him to return to his carriage, and to be off to the south of Ireland. It was some time before they discovered that, instead of the well-fed, old O'Connell, a young artist had fallen into their hands.*

The great industrialists and businessmen of Belfast looked to Britain and the Empire for markets and raw materials. They had more in common with their counterparts in Merseyside and Clydeside than they did with the rest of Ireland. The Mayor Sir Edward Cowan was able to congratulate the Town Council in 1882 that while trade was depressed in Dublin, in the course of the previous year 1,500 new buildings had been erected, with fifty nine new streets and that the valuation of the town had more than doubled in twenty years. 'It is, I think', he declared 'highly creditable that while many other districts of the country were more or less disturbed, Belfast enjoyed such exceptional peace and quiet'. As the south and west of the country pressed for a parliament in Dublin, Belfast's strongly Protestant and Unionist majority made preparations to resist Irish Home Rule by force. Sir Edward Cowan reminded his counterparts in Dublin that Belfast, with a large proportion of the population and so much of the wealth, would have a say about the future and that such 'a large town, backed by so large a part of the province, forms and must form an important factor, which will have to be taken into consideration by those who call out for Home Rule, Nationalism, and Ireland for the Irish'. By 1912, Belfast had become the centre of opposition to Home Rule for Ireland, and within a year an army, the Ulster Volunteer Force, had been formed to underline its determination to resist its imposition at all costs. A century of religious conflict had begun.

Chapter 4

RELIGION

There are few countries in Western Europe where the Church, of various denominations, has had such a profound impact on the lives of local people than in Ireland. In the early nineteenth century the three major denominations, Roman Catholic, Anglican and Presbyterian, between them accounted for all but a very small proportion of the Irish population. In 1861 only 146 people described themselves as being of no religion, or else atheists, freethinkers, deists, materialists or in some other term implying a rejection of conventional religious belief. Even then, the census commissioners were at pains to point out that of the 72 persons returned as being of 'no religion' seven 'were children under five years of age, and presumed to be unable to answer for themselves'.

From 1537 until 1870 and disestablishment, the Church of Ireland was the state church in Ireland. It had had close doctrinal and disciplinary ties with the Church of England since the Anglo-Norman invasion, and these had been strengthened by the Reformation. Under the Act of Union, 1800, the Church of Ireland was united with the Church of England, and this united church was declared to be the established church of the United Kingdom of Great Britain and Ireland. Nevertheless, the Church of Ireland remained administratively separate; from the Reformation, apart from the reign of Queen Mary (1553–8), the Church of Ireland was under the ecclesiastical jurisdiction of the Archbishop of Armagh, primate of all Ireland, and the bishops of the dioceses, all of whom were appointed by the Crown.

Although it was initially committed to spreading Protestantism to the native Irish population, its congregations were made up mostly of English and Scottish settlers and officials. The vast majority of landowners were Anglican and, outside Ulster, its membership consisted mostly of the professional classes. Fifty per cent or more of all barristers, solicitors, civil engineers, medical men, architects and bankers are listed in the 1861 census as members of the Church of Ireland. Unlike the Church of England, which claimed to represent the majority of Englishmen, the Church of Ireland embraced only a minority of the population – no more than 12 per cent according to the census returns of 1861.

By the beginning of the eighteenth century the Anglican Church was in a state of serious decay. The wars of the seventeenth century had damaged many churches, the bishops' palaces and parsonage houses had been ruined, and many of the clergy were non-resident. Robert Mossom, Bishop of Derry, describing the conditions in his diocese in a memorial which he addressed to the Irish Society in 1670, declared that, except within the city itself, there was not a single church that was fit for God's worship, and that 'the Holy Offices' were being administered either in 'dirty cabins' or in 'common ale-houses'. Edward Wakefield, writing of Co. Waterford as late as 1812, declared that 'It is not unusual to see church walls grown green in the inside, and the clergyman dressed in a surplus covered with iron-mould spots, which perhaps had not been washed for twelve months, delivering a discourse to a congregation composed of from two to six persons.'

The church nevertheless was unpopular among dissenters and Catholics because of the imposition of the tithe system to support the Church of Ireland clergy. William Gladstone's Irish Church Act of 1869 dissolved the union between the churches of England and Ireland and ended the Church of Ireland's position as the established church. Before dis-establishment land rental and tithe charges had been the major source of revenue. Tithes now ceased altogether to be paid and most of the church lands were alienated. Its property was vested in a body of Commissioners, known as the Commissioners of Church Temporalities in Ireland, which was empowered to lend money to the tenants to enable them to purchase their land. After 1869 the major sources of revenue were returns on investments and voluntary contributions. This led to a dramatic fall in episcopal incomes and marked the beginning of a decline in the Church of Ireland's status.

Roman Catholicism was, and remains, the overwhelmingly predominant creed in Ireland. Dr John Forbes, who toured Ireland in the middle of the nineteenth century, commented:

> *My experience in Ireland, hitherto, had certainly been almost entirely that of a man travelling in a Catholic country; so small a portion of the whole field of observation did the Protestant element seem to occupy: and ... this decided Catholic character assumes even a still more striking aspect when presented in its Sunday dress.*

In 1861 Catholics made up a minority of the population in four Ulster counties (Antrim, Armagh, Down and Londonderry) as well as in the towns of Belfast and Carrickfergus. In two other Ulster counties, Fermanagh and Tyrone, they accounted for not much more than half the population. Elsewhere in Ireland Catholics were everywhere a substantial majority, making up 86 per cent of the population in Leinster, and more than 90 per cent in both Munster and Connacht. The Commissioners of

Open-air mass in penal times.

Public Instruction calculated that 80.9 per cent of the population was Roman Catholic in 1834. After 1845, it was the Catholic population which suffered most severely from the effects of Famine and of post-Famine emigration. The first true census of religion, taken in 1861, suggested that the number of Catholics had fallen by 30 per cent since 1834.

The dedication of Irish Catholics to the church was remarked upon by numerous travellers. In 1887, Paschel Grousset, an exiled French journalist, noted that the Catholics he met were 'Catholics not so only in name. The greater number follow the services of the Church, observe all the rites, maintain a direct and constant intercourse with priests. The sincerity of their faith is particularly striking, and is not to be found in the same degree even in Italy or in Spain.' Dr John Forbes visited two Catholic chapels in Limerick, St Michael's and St John's, in 1852 both in the morning and afternoon during the time of service. He was impressed by the fervour of the congregation:

> *It was a striking sight, and not a little touching, to see those children of poverty at their devotions; kneeling, crouching, many stretched at full length upon the ground, as if dead; others striking their breasts, or holding up their hands fixedly in the air, or counting their beads; and all uttering their responses in the most earnest tones, – all apparently in that profound absorption of the faculties, which indicates utter oblivion of everything external. Many children were present, and exhibited as much fervour of devotion as their seniors. A few of the women had books, more had rosaries, but the majority had neither.*

The predominant place enjoyed by the Catholic Church in Ireland is all the more remarkable when one takes into account the series of enactments of the late seventeenth and early eighteenth centuries which were designed to undermine its position. After the Treaty of Limerick in 1691 the Irish Parliament, filled with Protestant landowners and controlled from England, enacted a penal code that secured and enlarged the landlords' holdings and degraded and impoverished the Irish Catholics. As a result of these harsh laws, Catholics could neither teach their children nor send them abroad; persons of property could not enter into mixed marriages; Catholic property was inherited equally among the sons unless one was a Protestant, in which case he received everything; a Catholic could not inherit property if there was any Protestant heir; a Catholic could not possess arms or a horse worth more than £5; Catholics could not hold leases for more than thirty-one years, and they could not make a profit greater than a third of their rent. The hierarchy of the Catholic Church was banished or suppressed, and Catholics could not hold seats in the Irish Parliament, hold public office, vote or practise law.

Had the laws been ruthlessly put into effect there would soon have been an end to the organized practice of Catholicism. Instead the laws were sporadically enforced in the seventeenth century and largely ignored in the eighteenth century. The laws affecting property were the most stringently executed, so that most of those Catholic families that owned land eventually became Protestant. Uncertainty of tenure discouraged investment in land improvement and led to the cutting of timber for immediate profit. Catholics found a profitable field in trade, and many made fortunes in the seaport towns. Other Catholics conformed in order to practise at the bar or to become solicitors. As the Catholic landed class diminished in numbers and influence, they were more and more cut off from the social life of the countryside.

Thurles Chapel. Illustrated London News *(1848).*

Despite the penal laws, most of the cities and towns outside Ulster had their Catholic chapels. Many of the Dublin chapels were at first merely converted stables and storehouses, but by the beginning of the second quarter of the eighteenth century new chapels were being built, almost all of them close together in the lanes and back streets along the Liffey.

Priests retained tremendous influence over their flocks, as noted by Frenchman De Latocnaye in the 1790s:

They are, in fact, the judges of the country and settle everything connected with morals and manners. They excommunicate a peasant and oblige him to leave a parish. Great care, then, must be taken not to displease them, and especially care must be taken that they get their dues.

The life of a rural priest was a hard one, nevertheless, as Dr John Forbes noted in 1852:

Generally speaking, the style of living of the rural priests, whether parish priests or curates, is hardly what would be called in England genteel or even comfortable; partly in consequence of their scanty revenues, and partly, perhaps, on account of the comparatively isolated and lower social position they occupy. Unlike the clergy of England, whether Protestant or Catholic, the priests in Ireland are permitted to hold but rare social intercourse with the gentry in their own neighbourhoods – greatly, I should say, to the discredit of the gentry, and greatly to the loss of the community ... I own I was surprised to find, in my limited intercourse with the priests of both degrees, how well they preserved the character of gentlemen, both in their manners and external appearance. I found them always well-dressed, very polite, and with the conversation of men who had been well-educated.

Presbyterianism came to Ireland from Scotland with the first plantation of Ulster during the early seventeenth century. The Presbyterian population was heavily concentrated in Ulster, where 96 per cent of its members lived. In the counties of Antrim and Down, and in Belfast and Carrickfergus, Presbyterians were the largest single religious group, while they were also well represented in Co. Londonderry. Congregations of Presbyterian settlers were also established during the Cromwellian period at Athlone, Clonmel, Dublin, Limerick and Mullingar.

In the first half of the seventeenth century the Church of Ireland contained several Scottish bishops who were prepared to ordain men of strong Calvinist theology and several of them served in the parishes of the estates owned by Hamilton and Montgomery in Down and Antrim. After the Restoration, nonconforming ministers were removed from parishes of the Church of Ireland, but the Irish administration could not afford to alienate such a substantial Protestant population and Presbyterianism was allowed to continue in the country, with the stipends of ministers paid through the *regium donum* – literally 'the King's gift'.

Despite their support for the Williamite cause in Ireland during the 1690s, the government and bishops soon renewed their attack on the Presbyterian Church. Their freedom of action was severely curtailed by the penal laws so that it was technically illegal for Presbyterian ministers to perform marriages for members of their congregation until 1782 and it was not until 1845 that they could legally marry a Presbyterian and a member of the Church of Ireland. It is hardly surprising therefore to find that Presbyterians consistently made up the majority of emigrants from Ulster to colonial America, while many of those who remained in Ireland became prominent in movements for reform culminating in the revolt of the United Irishmen in 1798.

The eighteenth century saw significant tensions within the Synod of Ulster, which was divided between the Old Lights and the New Lights. The Old Lights were conservative Calvinists who believed that ministers and ordinands should subscribe to the Westminster Confession of Faith. The New Lights were more liberal, were unhappy with the Westminster Confession and did not require ministers to subscribe to it. The New Lights dominated the Synod of Ulster during the eighteenth century, allowing the more conservative Scottish Presbyterian dissenters, Seceders and Convenanters to establish a strong presence in Ulster and the great majority of Ulster Presbyterians united in 1840 to form the General Assembly of the Presbyterian Church of Ireland. By the middle of the nineteenth century the leading Presbyterian cleric Dr Henry Cooke played a major role in weaning the Presbyterians of Ulster away from their old alliance with the Liberals and Catholics against the Anglican Establishment, and substituting a new alliance with the Unionist Episcopalians against the Catholics.

The Commissioners of Public Instruction in 1834 recorded a total of only 21, 808 persons of other denominations, although this, they noted, excluded a considerable number of Wesleyan Methodists 'who, although attending religious service in other places of worship, consider themselves to be in connection with the Established Church, and wished to be classed as members of that body'. One of the most prominent of the groups outside the three main denominations was the Religious Society of Friends, also known as 'Quakers' or 'Friends', which originated in the north-west of England during the mid-seventeenth century. The Quaker movement was brought to Ireland by William Edmundson when he established a business in Dublin in 1652. Outside Dublin the Quakers were thickly settled in a few areas. The initial concentrations were: in Ulster at Grange, Richhill, Lurgan and Lisburn; the richer agricultural areas in central Leinster; the isolated small urban centres like Wicklow and Carlow; and the major coastal trading cities such as Dublin, Cork, Waterford and Limerick.

They came into conflict with the authorities over their refusal to serve in the militia, to take oaths and to pay tithes. Most of the early Quakers were engaged in agriculture and the linen trade; later persecution for not paying tithes discouraged them from continuing as farmers. By the mid-eighteenth century most Irish Quakers were artisans, shop-keepers, merchants and professional people. Some Quaker manufacturers became household names, like Jacobs the biscuit-makers and Bewleys who established a chain of cafes in Dublin from 1840. In 1780 Arthur Young declared them 'the only wealthy traders in Ireland'. William Savery, an American Quaker, and notable preacher, toured through Ireland in 1797 and 1798 and wrote in his journal: 'Friends in Ireland seem to live like Princes of the Earth, more than in any country I have seen – their gardens, horses, carriages, and various conveniences, with abundance of their tables, appeared to me to call for much more gratitude and humility, than in some instances it is to be feared is the case.'

It is ironic, given the country's reputation for religious conflict, that many groups fled to Ireland in search of religious toleration. The Moravians had their origin in a pre-Reformation Protestant church called the *Unitas Fratrum* or United Brethern, a Hussite movement which arose in Moravia and Bohemia in what is now the Czech Republic. Arriving in Ireland in 1746 when the first Moravian Church was founded in Dublin, they spread northwards in the succeeding years, preaching with considerable success in Antrim, Armagh, Derry and other counties. There were soon societies in most Ulster counties.

Jews have lived in Ireland since at least the Middle Ages. Dublin had a rabbi by 1700 and a Jewish cemetery opened in 1718. By the middle of the eighteenth century Cork also had an organized community. Proposals to permit their naturalization were debated in the Irish Parliament on four occasions between 1743 and 1747 but were rejected on each occasion. The Irish Naturalisation Act of 1784 explicitly excluded Jews, a provision only repealed in 1816. By that year there were said to be only two Jewish families in Dublin. From the 1820s a new Jewish population appeared, mostly of German and Polish origin but coming to Ireland via England. They included a high proportion of goldsmiths, silversmiths and watchmakers and merchants. Their numbers remained small, with only 393 Jews in 1861 and 285 in 1871. From the 1880s they were reinforced from Eastern Europe, mainly because of persecution in Tsarist Russia, and between 1861 and 1901 the population rose from less than 400 to almost 4,000, of whom over half were to be found in Dublin.

Savage religious persecution in their native France drove French Calvinists, known as Huguenots, to emigrate in large numbers. Some 10,000 made their way to Ireland where they were welcomed by the Ascendancy for their Protestantism and for their industry and because they strengthened the Protestant community. An Act of 1692 'for encouragement of protestant strangers' specifically allowed such strangers (who did not include Scots) to worship 'in their own several rites used in their own countries'. This was a departure from the practice of Charles II's reign, when they had been required to worship according to the rites of the established church. In some of the Huguenot churches ministers were conformist and used French versions of the Book of Common Prayer, but others were nonconformist and maintained a Calvinist form of worship.

The largest Huguenot community was in Dublin, where there were four French churches, two conformist and two nonconformist. The community included weavers, silk workers, goldsmiths and traders of various kinds. When the Huguenot regiments were disbanded after the Treaty of Ryswick over 500 officers obtained pensions on the Irish establishment.

Many of them settled at Portarlington, where Henri de Ruvigny, Earl of Galway, had obtained a grant of forfeited land. They became tradesmen – butchers, bakers, smiths, carpenters, tailors and shoemakers – and linen manufacture was carried on a small scale. The most important Huguenot settlement in Ulster was founded in Lisburn (Lisnagarvey). William III's Bill to foster the linen trade in 1697 resulted in more than seventy French families, led by Louis Crommelin, establishing the industry in Lisburn. For three or four generations they sustained themselves as a distinctive group but were gradually absorbed into the greater community.

The seventeenth and eighteenth centuries also saw many leave Germany for England in search of religious freedom. One of the most unusual migrations of populations occurred at the beginning of the eighteenth century. The 'Poor Palatines' as they became known, due to the fact that they were destitute, left their Rhineland homes for England during the bitter winter of 1708/9. Unpopular in London, some 800 families were deported to Ireland in 1709. The main settlements were in Co. Limerick and Co. Kerry. An allowance of 40s. a year to each family for seven years was provided by the government in 1712 and this was extended for fourteen years in 1718. The Palatines grew flax and hemp and they conformed to the established church, but the commissioners pointed out that they needed a minister to read the service in German and an agent who could speak their language to see that they were not misused by the landlords or their Irish neighbours As late as 1840 Mr and Mrs Hall, who were touring Ireland, described the Palatines as 'different in character, and district in habits from the people in the country'. They found that 'the elders of the family preserve in a great degree the language, customs, and religion of their old country; but the younger mingle and marry with their Irish neighbours'. Through intermarriage with their neighbours they eventually disappeared as a separate element in the population.

Amongst the larger religious denominations in Ireland, such integration proved impossible, particularly in the north-east of the country. For much of its early history Belfast was a major centre of Protestantism in Ireland. It was recorded in 1707 that there were not 'above seven Papists (in the town) and . . . not above 150 Papists in the whole Barony'. It was not until 1784 that the town's first official Catholic chapel was opened in Crooked (now Chapel) Lane, thanks partly to a subscription from Protestants of £84 towards its construction.

By the early years of the nineteenth century Catholics formed about one-sixth of the population of Belfast, the majority of them located in the area close to the chapel in Crooked Lane. Relations between the two communities was already in decline however. One factor was rural migration which from the 1820s to the middle of the century was mainly Catholic. By 1850 Catholics formed one-third of the population, as the town was filled by families fleeing the effect of the Great Famine. As Belfast's population grew, clashes between the different religious groups became an increasing feature of life in the town. Sectarian rivalry manifested itself in waves of rioting beginning with a clash on 12 July 1813 and continuing throughout the nineteenth and twentieth centuries.

Religious rivalries were also a constant problem in many parts of rural Ulster from the late eighteenth century. It was in the tiny farms of these areas where the linen industry flourished that increasing competition for land once thought uneconomic resulted in faction fighting at local fairs and markets. This intensified with the development of rival organizations which had the dual purpose of defending co-religionists and intimidating religious opponents. Defenderism, a secret society that emerged in the rural areas of Co. Armagh among the Catholic population during the 1780, carried out a number of attacks against Protestants; these generally took the form of late night armed raids with little loss of life or destruction of property. In September 1795 a large Defender force from several Ulster counties attacked Protestants near Loughgall, Co. Armagh. Their defeat, at what subsequently became known as the Battle of the Diamond, was a major impetus to the formation of the first Orange lodges. The Order was modelled on the Freemasons and their oath went: 'I ... do solemnly swear that I will, to the utmost of my power, support and defend the King and his heirs as long as he or they support the Protestant ascendancy'. Despite early government attempts to suppress the organization, it remained the largest Protestant organization in Ireland and still holds its annual 12 July demonstrations at around twenty venues across Northern Ireland.

In Dublin, and many other towns in the south and west, Catholic and Protestant communities were not segregated as they were in Belfast, but they tended to live separate lives. Schools, hospitals, and other charitable institutions, voluntary organizations, even sporting clubs, tended to be organized along denominational lines. Novelist Elizabeth Bowan, in her memoirs of childhood in middle-class Edwardian Ireland wrote: 'I took the existence of Roman Catholicism for granted but met few and was not interested in them. They were simply – the others, whose world lay alongside ours but never touched.'

Religious tensions could arise at the most unlikely places. According to the *Irish Times*, 6 January 1875 the following incident took place at Menlo, a small village on the outskirts of Galway:

> *As the remains of the late Sir Thomas Blake, of Meale Castle, were being conveyed last evening for internment to the Menlo churchyard, some rumours were afloat on the way that a scene would ensue, and a subsequent portion of the proceedings served to realise their anticipations. The remains were borne to the churchyard by the tenantry, but as soon was the cortege reached the gate leading to the enclosure, a proposal was made to carry the remains to a portion of the ground set apart for Roman Catholics. This was forcibly resisted by the Protestants present, and a long and fierce struggle followed. The Rev. Mr O'Sullivan and other Protestant gentlemen were abused, and some of them assaulted. The Protestants were determined that he should be buried with the funeral rites of their Church; but the Catholic tenantry were much more numerous, and showed as much determination on the other side. All the available constabulary force of the town were turned out to the scene, and it was with difficulty that even this power could preserve order. Finally the remains were interred, and the funeral service got through.*

Chapter 5

PRIMARY EDUCATION

M any travellers to Ireland remarked upon the Irish peasantry's love of learning. 'Education', wrote Edward Wakefield in the early nineteenth century,

> *is more general among the poorer classes in Ireland than it is among the same description of persons in England. In the former the peasantry are more quick of comprehension than the latter. Labourers in England can plough the land or make a fence in a manner which would astonish the Irish, but they are so boorishly stupid that it is difficult to converse with them and they seldom trouble themselves about anything beyond the precincts of their own parish. But the Irish, with less skill in manual operations, possess more intelligence, they are shrewd by nature, and have a most anxious desire to obtain information.*

Statutory provision for a system of education in Ireland had been in existence since the sixteenth century. In 1537 Henry VIII aimed to end 'the certain savage and wild kind and manner of living' of the Irish by providing for the establishment of elementary schools in each parish, the prime purpose of which was the teaching of the English language. Nevertheless, the task of organizing and maintaining the parish schools had been assigned to the Anglican clergy who, being usually poor and non-resident, found it impossible to overcome local hostility. Bishop

Nicholson of Carlisle, who later became Bishop of Derry, complained in 1714 that the poor in Ireland still spoke Irish and that they were not sending their children to the parish schools mainly because the school-master expected payment which they were unable to make.

While the penal laws were enforced, Irish peasants were forced to depend upon hedge schools for their elementary education. These were basically a collection of poor students and a teacher holding class in a ditch or hedgerow, with one of the pupils serving as a look-out for law officers. These were usually set up by itinerant schoolmasters who were paid according to the size of the school. They first appeared towards the end of the seventeenth century when wandering scholars found it necessary to hide themselves in remote places away from official view. Arthur Young, who travelled through Ireland in the 1770s, wrote of encountering 'many a ditch full of travellers'. As the penal laws were relaxed, the master was able to make himself and his pupils a bit more comfortable, settling in the comparative luxury of a sod hut or an unused barn for his classroom.

Most hedge masters taught the 'threes Rs' but because of the impediments to Catholic education few had been to universities or even to secondary schools. The quality of teaching varied enormously. In 1821 Bishop Doyle noted that the masters 'in many instances are extremely ignorant'. On the other hand, when Tommy Maher, who had for years taught in a mud hut at Goffs Bridge in Co. Wexford, transferred his allegiance to the Board of Education in 1815, an inspector was sent to examine his pupils. The inspector was amazed

> *at the skill of the twelve year old boys in reading the new books, and considering the possibility that they were reciting from memory, I invited one of their number to read me a passage from the Gospel of Saint Matthew. Evidently the child misunderstood me. He searched in his satchel until he found his tattered book, stood up, and proceeded to read me the account of Christ's passion – in Greek.*

The best estimates indicate that in the mid-1820s 300,000–400,000 Catholic children were being educated at parental expense, a remarkable testimony to the peasantry's enthusiasm for schooling. German traveller,

Johann Kohl visited one of the last of the old hedge schools during his stay in Ireland in the 1840s:

> *The schoolhouse was a mud hovel, covered with green sods, without windows or any other comforts. The little pupils, wrapped up as well as their rags would cover them, sat beside the low open door, towards which they were all holding their books in order to obtain a portion of the scanty light it admitted . . . The school-house stood close by the roadside, but many of the children resided several miles off, and even the schoolmaster did not live near it. At a certain hour they all met here; and when the day's task is over the boys put their primers in their pockets and scamper off home; whilst the schoolmaster fastens the door as well as he can, puts his turf fees into his bag, takes his stick and trudges off to his remote cottage across the bog.*

As the penal laws relaxed in the late eighteenth century, a number of religious orders devoted themselves to the education of the Catholic poor. Catherine McAuley opened her first house of the Sisters of Mercy in Baggot Street, Dublin, in 1828. By 1850 there were 3,000 sisters

Irish schoolmaster. Illustrated London News *(1857).*

committed to education in several towns. The Brigidine Sisters, the Loreto Sisters, the Irish Sisters of Charity and the Holy Faith Sisters were all devoted to education and these native foundations were assisted by Irish houses of Ursulines, Dominicans and Sisters of St Louis. Edmund Ignatius Rice established the first Irish Christian Brothers school in Carrick-on-Suir in 1816, and by 1867 there were fifty-five Christian Brothers schools across Ireland.

An alternative to hedge schools or those founded by religious orders was provided by various Protestant societies for the conversion of Roman Catholics. The Irish charity school movement began in the early eighteenth century under voluntary auspices. In most cases the charity schools enrolled both Protestant and Catholic children, but permitted instruction only in the Protestant faith. In 1717 the Society in Dublin for Promoting Christian Knowledge was formed under the leadership of Dr Henry Maule, later Protestant bishop of Meath, and by 1725 the society was operating 163 schools containing 3,000 pupils.

A similar society was known as the 'charter school society', from the charter of George III (6 February 1734) by which the Incorporated Society in Dublin for Promoting English Protestant Schools in Ireland was established. It was specified that 'the children of the Popish and other poor natives' were to be instructed in the English tongue and the formularies of the established Church of Ireland. It aimed to provide a means of educating the children of Catholics 'before the corruptions of popery have taken root in their hearts', and to produce Protestant wives for English settlers who in the past had married Catholics because they had no choice. It was considered essential that the schools be boarding schools so that the children would be removed from the influence of their parents and priests. For this reason the schools were located in the more remote parts of the country.

The charter greatly aided the society in its fund-raising, and from 1738 to 1794 it also received £1,000 annually from successive kings. In 1747 the Irish Parliament granted the society the proceeds from the licensing duty on hawkers and pedlars, and parliamentary grants began in 1751 and continued until 1831. Most of the early schools were also endowed by prominent members of the gentry and church. The school at Dundalk, for example, was endowed in 1738 by Lord Limerick. The children were also employed by a local company manufacturing cambric in which Lord

Limerick had a financial interest. The schools laid great emphasis on manual labour and, according to the society's records, each school was provided with a sundial and an hourglass to regulate the children's work. The boys were employed chiefly on agricultural work and the girls at housecrafts. In Newtown Corry (Monaghan) the children were employed making coarse linen for export to the West Indies.

Masters were appointed to the schools with very small salaries which they augmented by selling the produce of the child's labour. A description of the masters given by a critical supporter of the schools in 1806 gives an impression of the quality of teaching. Teachers were described as:

> *Men of vulgar habits, course manners, often ignorant in the extreme of everything but the common rudiments of reading, writing and arithmetic, exhibiting nothing in conduct or example that could raise the minds of the children above the level of that semi-barbarism which has been the character of the lower class of the people of this country.*

This impression was confirmed by John Howard, the prison reformer, who inspected the schools in 1784 and in 1787. 'The children, in general', he averred, 'were sickly, pale, and such miserable objects, that they were a disgrace to all society; and their reading had been neglected for the purpose of making them work for the masters'.

There were never more than sixty or so charter schools in existence at any one time. A series of private and public inquiries, culminating in the disclosures of the Irish Education Inquiry of 1825, revealed extensive cruelty and neglect, and shortly afterwards state support was withdrawn. There was a great deal of Catholic opposition to these charity schools. This is hardly surprising if we take a look at the books distributed to the schools, which bore titles such as *The hazard of being saved in the Church of Rome and Discourse against Transubstantiation together with a discourse showing the Protestant way to Heaven.*

The Society for the Education of the Poor in Ireland, better known as the Kildare Place Society, was founded in 1811 and aimed to provide a system of interdenominational education. Its objective was

> *the admission of pupils, uninfluenced by religious distinctions, and the reading of the Bible or Testament, without note or comment, by*

all the pupils who had attained a suitable proficiency; excluding catechisms and controversial treatises; the Bible or Testament not to be used as a class book from which children should be taught to read or spell.

In 1812 commissioners appointed to inquire into the state of the schools and charities of public foundation recommended that 'no attempt should be made to influence or disturb the peculiar religious tenets of any sect or description of Christians'.

For a time it had the approval of the Catholic clergy and laymen. Daniel O'Connell was on the society's board of governors, Catholic clergy became patrons of individual schools, and the clergy gave their cautious sanction to the society's activities. Educationally, the society was a considerable success, publishing the first major series of sequential textbooks in the British Isles, establishing model schools for the training of teachers and pioneering the creation of an efficient system of school inspection. By 1820 the society was operating 381 schools, enrolling 26,474 pupils.

In 1820, however, the Kildare Place Society abandoned its neutral stance and began to allocate part of its income to the schools of various Protestant proselytizing societies, such as the London Hibernian Society, the Baptist Society and the Association for Discountenancing Vice. Simultaneously, Protestant clergy and lay patrons violated with increasing boldness the society's rules prohibiting the denominational exposition of the scripture readings. O'Connell resigned in 1820 and led an agitation against the society. A petition signed by the leading Catholic bishops led in 1824 to the establishment of another official inquiry into Irish popular education. In 1830 the parliament grant was finally withdrawn and the number of schools quickly declined.

It was against this background of haphazard education and falling standards of living that the Irish system of National Education was founded in 1831 under the direction of the Chief Secretary, E G Stanley. The national schools which resulted were built with the aid of the Commissioners of National Education and local trustees. The national system of primary education established in 1831 antedates by almost a full four decades the establishment of a similar system in England. The curriculum was to be secular in content, though provision was made for

Woodwork class, Middletown, 1913. The Allison Collection, PRONI.

separate religious instruction at special stated times. The board gave assistance to local committees in building schools and made a major contribution towards the teachers' salaries. A teacher-training school was established in Dublin and model schools were set up gradually throughout the county.

Mr and Mrs Hall, who remembered the old school-houses as 'for the most part, wretched hovels, in which the boys and girls mixed indiscriminately', were impressed by the transformation brought about by the Board of Education. 'The school-houses, instead of being dark, close, dirty and unwholesome, are neat and commodious buildings, well-ventilated and in all respects healthful.' They were also impressed with the books supplied by the board. These included 'an English Grammar, Arithmetic books for various classes; books on geometry, book keeping; An Introduction to the Art of Reading and a Treatise on Mensuration.'

German traveller Johann Kohl, who visited an Irish national school in Wexford in the 1840s, declared:

> *The one I visited at Wexford, like most of the Irish infant schools had only been established five years, and contained ninety-one*

Catholic and thirty Protestant children. The children usually remain until their twelfth year, but the Catholics often send their daughters back again, as they are dissatisfied with the parochial schools which are attended by those of a more advance age … The system of education at these infant schools is very peculiar, and, indeed extremely poetical. All the instruction is conveyed in verses, which are sung by the little pupils, and, whenever it is possible, accompanied with a pantomimic acting of the subject. Almost every general movement made by the children is attended with singing. For instance, as they come into the schoolroom they sing the following verse:

> *We'll go to our places, and make no wry faces,*
> *And say all our lessons distinctly and slow;*
> *For if we don't do it, our mistress will know it,*
> *And into the corner we surely shall go.*

As well as receiving an education, girls were taught needlework and the National Education Board encouraged the teaching of agriculture and gardening to boys and girls. The priorities of the Commissioners of National Education are indicated in a set of instructions given to inspectors in 1836:

> *He [the inspector] will ascertain the advancement of education among the children, noting the proportion of children who can read fluently; what progress they have made in writing and arithmetic; whether any be taught geography, grammar, book-keeping and mensuration; whether girls be taught sewing or knitting.*

Although by the end of the nineteenth century free elementary schooling was provided for all children, the numbers attending schools in many areas was sparse. In 1852 Dr John Forbes found that attendance at school varied from place to place. At Kenmare, although there were 54 boys on the books, only 27 were present on the day he paid his visit. He was told that numbers had dropped because of recent emigration and due to the demands of the present harvest season. Although Acts of 1876 and 1880 prohibited the employment of children under 10 years old and children up to 13 were required to attend school, the Reports of the Commission for Education make it clear that many children made only infrequent attendance at school. In his general report into the Armagh Circuit in 1903 Mr Murphy commented that:

> *The character of the attendance remains practically unchanged. The same causes are at work in town and in country and the same unsatisfactory results are noticeable. In rural districts the pupils attend for the most part very irregularly. This is due to the demand for child labour, and partly to a seeming inability on the part of parents to appreciate the injustice they do to their children, when they keep them from school without sufficient reason.*

The main criticism of the new system came from the churches. The established church remained suspicious of these attempts to remove their influence over the education system. In 1839 the Church Education Society was established. Its declared object was to maintain an independent system of schools conducted under the auspices of the established church. By 1850 it had 1,800 schools affiliated to it but by the 1870s the expense of maintaining the society drove it into the state system. For a short time in the 1830s the Presbyterian Synod of Ulster also refused to have anything to do with the Education Board. Presbyterians were concerned at the restrictions placed on the use of the Bible, the limited rights of ministers of denominations different from that of the majority of the pupils. Gradually the board agreed to compromise on the points at issue and by the middle of the Victorian period Presbyterians were receiving grant aid for what was in fact virtually a self-contained system of denominational schools.

Ironically, the Roman Catholic clergy remained suspicious of what they continued to see as a proselytizing organization. The system at first enjoyed the support of the majority of bishops. Opposition soon emerged among a minority, most prominent of whom was Dr McHale, Bishop of Tuam from 1836. He believed that the scheme was anti-Catholic and anti-national and argued that education for Irish Catholics should be characteristically Irish and exclusively Catholic. A papal decision in 1841 allowed each bishop to decide whether the schools in his diocese might participate in the national school system.

The attitudes of the churches eventually led, in practice, to denominational schools under the control of clerical managers from the different religious bodies. In Catholic schools the manager was almost always the

Grange School, Co. Armagh, 1903. The Allison Collection, PRONI.

parish priest, and in Protestant schools the rector, minister or landlord. He was charged with the daily oversight of the school: he had the right to appoint and dismiss teachers who were to be hired from model or training schools established by the board; he chose which of the several approved sets of textbooks the school would use and, within broad limits, arranged the school's timetable.

The success of local schools was trumpeted in local newspapers. Readers of the *Belfast News Letter* on Friday 20 August 1858 were informed that:

> *The annual examination of Anahilt National School, near Hills-borough, was held on Friday, the 6th instant, in presence of the patron, the Rev. Thomas Greer, the committee, and a large number of respectable teachers and visitors. The examination lasted from half-past eleven A.M. till half-past four P.M. The prompt and correct answers of the pupils in the various classes delighted all present, and though time did not permit the examiners to test the capability of the children, ample opportunity was afforded to convince all present of the great excellence of this institution.*

In an effort to drive up standards, the Powis Commission of 1868–70 was responsible for introducing a system of payments by results, or the results system as it was called, into the national schools. According to evidence given to the Commission, only 33.5 per cent of pupils made an annual attendance of 100 days, and 50–65 per cent in some counties were found unable to read or write. These and other considerations led to the system of payment by results from 1872. Every pupil was examined in reading, writing and arithmetic. Those in third standard were examined in grammar and geography as well. In fourth and higher standards, pupils faced tests in agriculture, and girls in second and all higher standards were examined in needlework. To be eligible for examination a pupil had to have made 100 attendances during the year. The inspector examined each pupil and awarded a mark – number 1 pass, or number 2, or 0 for failure. The Education Office then worked out from these marks the amount of the payments to be made.

By the 1870s the number of schools had risen to 6,806, with 998,999 children in attendance. Although the average attendance was less than half the number on the rolls during the first forty years, literacy levels in Ireland rose. In 1841, 53 per cent of the population of 5 years of age and upwards was listed as illiterate. This was down to 33 per cent by 1871 and dropped to 18 per cent by 1891. Contemporaries noted that most children left school with the ability to read a newspaper, even if 'with difficulty'. The letters from emigrants, the signatures on marriage registers replacing the earlier 'X' and the increase in the number of threatening notices and letters issued during the land war of 1879–81 were some indications that the national schools had played a major role in the advancement of literacy in Ireland.

Chapter 6

INDUSTRY – WORKING LIFE

The Industrial Revolution did not have the same dramatic impact in Ireland as it did in Britain during the late eighteenth century. Ireland's proximity to Britain, then the first industrial nation in the world, was a crucial factor in her economic problems. The selling price of mass-produced British goods was so much cheaper than the corresponding Irish goods. Improved transportation systems within Ireland with the development of the canals, and later the coming of the railways, only made this situation worse. The only exception was the north-east of Ulster where industrial processes improved the productivity of the linen, cotton and shipbuilding industries. By the end of the nineteenth century many of these firms, such as Harland & Wolff, had become world famous.

The success of the various canals constructed between 1730 and the arrival of the railways did much to shape the development of trade, industry and population in Ireland. Before the eighteenth century badly maintained roads were the only means of travel. Several proposals to build canals in Ireland were made from 1690 onwards, but it was not until 1731 that work began on the Newry Canal, linking one of the country's leading ports with the inland basin around Lough Neagh by means of a cut connecting Carlingford Lough with the Upper Bann, near Portadown. Newry became an important port that served much of mid-Ulster and for a time the town competed with Belfast as the commercial capital of the North.

Harland & Wolff Shipyard with Titanic, *c.1911. Welch Collection, Ulster Museum.*

Canals were largely constructed in the rest of Ireland in the hope that they would create and stimulate traffic, as they had done in Britain. Few developed sufficient trade to justify the colossal expense. The Grand and Royal Canals soon developed a flourishing passenger service, with canal boats making their way from Dublin to the Shannon at a leisurely pace. On the Grand Canal, hotels were built for passengers at Portobello (Dublin), Sallins, Robertstown, Tullamore and Shannon Harbour. The Royal Canal had four passenger boats in regular service taking passengers from Dublin to Mullingar, a distance of fifty-three miles, taking thirteen and a half hours. Because of the slowness of canal travel each boat was equipped with facilities for serving meals on board. According to one traveller who journeyed on the Grand Canal in 1803, meals consisted of 'a leg of boiled mutton, a turkey, ham, vegetables, porter, and a pint of wine each, at four shillings and ten pence a head'. A German visitor in 1842 commented: 'As there are no railways in Ireland, with the exception of two miniature ones ... the canals which transverse the country are much used for travelling, and boats, generally full to overflowing, ply regularly from and to Dublin. The boats, like the *trekschits* in Holland, are drawn by horses that move along at a smart trot.'

The slowness of travel by canal proved fatal to its commercial viability during the great industrial expansion of the Victorian era and by the 1840s, and the coming of the railways, the canal age was effectively over. With the railways regular travel opened up to all but the very poorest. The first railway to be authorized in Ireland was the Limerick and Waterford which obtained parliamentary approval in 1826. However, it was not until December 1834 that the first Irish railway was open for business. It was the six-mile-long Dublin and Kingstown Railway and it opened up the coastal area south of Dublin for residential development. Its contractor William Dargan became the 'Father of the Irish Railways' and he was involved in the financing and building of most lines up to his death in 1867. Although the Dublin and Kingstown line was a success, investors were slow to put their money into railways, because there was not the same need for cheap, efficient transport as in heavily industrialized England.

Garvagh, Derry Central Railway, c.1905. Garvagh Branch Library.

In the more industrialized north-east, manufacturers set up the Ulster Railway Company which launched the second Irish line, between Belfast and Portadown, in 1842. In the south of Ireland the most important railway was the Great Southern and Western which linked Dublin and Cork in 1849. By 1850 some 700 miles of railway were open or under construction. Railways allowed Irish agriculture easier access to the huge English market. Social changes included the spread of national newspapers and the growth of seaside resorts. The railway opened up the interior of the country and, drawing remote areas into the mass market, was to have a profound impact on Irish life in the latter half of the nineteenth century.

Gangs of navvies were recruited from the canal and railway construction industry in England. It took a year on the railway to make a labourer into a navvy who could work a full day shifting 'muck', as the heavy clay was called. Many were extended families of workmen from different parts of Ireland and some were from Liverpool and Scotland. They were paid a piece-work rate, which was essentially earning according to the amount of muck they could shift, the quantity being assessed by overseers who measured the loads in wheelbarrows. An experienced navvy could shift about 20 tons of clay in a 12-hour day using a pick and shovel. He could put away two pounds of beef per day washed down with a dozen quarts of beer. Little wonder that their life expectancy was short. Navvies followed the work; few had settled wives with them, but they formed makeshift family groupings with the women who joined them in the encampments and shanty dwellings which grew up around the line of the railway. A clergyman, the Revd St George Sargent, recalled his parsonage at the Mendicity Institute in Dublin: 'I think they are the most neglected and spiritually destitute people I ever met . . . ignorant of Bible religion and gospel truth, infected with infidelity and very often with revolutionary principles.'

For much of its history Ireland has been a largely agricultural economy. A continuously expanding demand for Irish agricultural produce in the British market and high prices made the late eighteenth century and early nineteenth centuries boom years, encouraging Irish farmers to increase their output. From the 1770s there was a marked increase in tillage and the volume of corn exports which expanded yet further during the Napoleonic Wars. The increased tillage was accompanied by rising export of pigs, and the expansion of dairying was reflected in increasing exports of butter. From the 1820s, with the introduction of steam shipping between Ireland and Britain and the subsequent extension of the railways in both countries, there was a marked expansion in livestock exports.

The slump in agricultural prices after Waterloo seriously altered the prospects for Irish agriculture. Many farmers found it difficult to keep up payments of high rents and found themselves heavily in arrears. This in turn led to a rise in the tide of unemployment in both town and country. Many fled to the towns in search of work. This led to a great deal of bitterness, as labourers in the countryside were usually prepared to work for lower wages than their town counterparts, a situation that employers were only too happy to exploit.

In the countryside, women played an important role in bringing in extra money to the household. Spinning was traditionally regarded as women's work and for centuries Irish women spun wool and linen which was woven into cloth for family use. Yarn was sold in local markets and woollen yard was being exported to Britain by the first half of the eighteenth century. Wool spinning was concentrated in the southern part of Ireland, in Cos. Cork, Kilkenny and Tipperary. Although the 1841 census recorded that over 70,000 women were engaged in spinning wool, many of the 300,000 unspecified spinners may also have done so.

By the end of the eighteenth century linen spinning had spread from north-east Ulster through the remainder of the province into north Connacht and north Leinster. Most children were taught how to spin by their mothers; spinning wheels were not expensive and many were supplied free by the Linen Board. Wives and daughters of weavers supplied them with yarn and some weavers hired young live-in female servants to spin and to help with housework and farm chores. In many parts of Connacht and north Leinster a woman's income from spinning was more regular than a man's earnings from agricultural labour, and women often provided the main cash income for a household. An account of Donegal in 1739 maintained that 'The Farmer generally contents himself with no more Land than is necessary to feed his family; which he diligently tills; and Depends on the Industry of his Wife and Daughters to pay by their Spinning the Rent and Say [save?] up Riches'. Spinning was mechanized during the late eighteenth century, long before weaving.

Handloom weaver, Moria. WAG295.

Women and children formed most of the workforce of the water-powered cotton and woollen mills.

Weaving was a major source of employment until the early twentieth century in both the towns and the countryside. Weaving did not become mechanized as quickly as spinning, so when woollen and worsted spinning mills were erected in the late eighteenth and early nineteenth centuries, the increased amount of yarn that was produced continued to be woven at handlooms in cottages. Weaving became mechanized from the 1820s and 1830s and hand-weaving disappeared during the late nineteenth century. New machines and greater power changed the textile industry in Ulster from a home industry to one based in the factory. Instead of being scattered through the province, textile manufacture was now concentrated on Belfast, where imported fuel was cheaper, transport to and from the factory cost less, and there was no difficulty in attracting labour from the surrounding countryside.

The Industrial Revolution did not have the same impact on Dublin as it did on cities of similar size in Britain. The chief industrial wealth of

Dublin in the eighteenth century came from woollen manufacture. It had expanded rapidly with the opening of direct trade with North America, the main source of raw materials, and with the encouragement given by the Irish Parliament. The Dublin Parliament laid duties on all imported cottons, and gave large grants to private individuals to establish factories. English weavers were also encouraged to settle in the Liberties. The Dublin Society made grants for the purchase of new machinery and gave bounties on the sale of manufactured goods.

By about 1786 there are said to have been at least 1,600 cotton-weavers employed in Dublin. Although a fair amount was sent to the Colonies, most was used for home consumption. Lord Sheffield wrote in his *Observations on the Manufactures, Trade, and Present State of Ireland*, 1785:

> *The amount of the consumption of woollens in Ireland we cannot know, but it is very great; and perhaps, no country whatever, in proportion to the number of inhabitants, consumes so much. The lower ranks are covered with the clumsiest woollen drapery, and although the material may not be fine, there is abundance of it. Besides coat and waistcoat, the lower classes wear a great coat, both summer and winter, if it can possibly be got.*

By the beginning of the nineteenth century, however, the 300 looms still working in Dublin could not compete with the new English power looms and the industry in the south went into rapid decline.

In the north, the cotton manufacture remained strong, with employers enjoying the double advantage of sufficient capital to buy machinery and the proximity of cheap coal from Lancashire. The factories spun cotton by steam or water power; this mill yarn was then 'put out' to hand-loom weavers to be made into cloth. They could be fined for any flaws or for days overdue. They were in no position to object because they had become dependent on the mill owners for their livelihood. John Milford's mill in Winetavern Street was five storeys high and its 5,364 spindles and 24 carding machines were turned by a ten-horsepower engine. In 1811 the Revd Dubourdieu calculated that in the Belfast area there were 150,000 power-driven spindles making over 70 million hanks of cotton yard, and concluded 'that not less than 30,000 individuals derive a good support from the muslin and calico branches of this trade, taking in all the different departments'.

With the end of the Napoleonic Wars in 1815 the cotton industry was hit hard by a severe trade depression. Wages fell and by the mid-1820s one-third of the cotton weavers in Belfast and its neighbourhood were unemployed. Those in work had to work long hours for low pay. The *Belfast News Letter* reported in February 1830 that Ballymacarrett weavers were forced to live on Indian meal unfit for cattle and that they were reduced to skeletons from overwork and lack of sleep.

Already the cotton industry in the North was being eclipsed by the newly mechanized linen mills. Linen had been in use in Ireland since ancient times. By the eighteenth century linen had become the most important of Irish manufactures. It was free from the restrictions placed by the English government on other Irish industries and it received extensive grants from the Irish Parliament. In 1711 a Linen Board was established, composed, according to its own description, of 'people of the highest rank in both Houses of Parliament'. It established spinning schools, bought flax, sent out inspectors and gave prizes for weaving.

Ireland was especially suited both by climate and soil for the industry and the manufactures did good business with America. In the North in particular local gentry, such as Lord Moira and the Earl of Hillsborough, promoted the development of the industry on their estates. By the close of the century the finer branches of the trade, diaper and cambric, were boosted by the settlement of Huguenot exiles who settled in the vicinity of Lisburn, Lurgan and Belfast. Arthur Young, on a visit to Newtownards during the summer of 1776, noted that the domestic linen industry employed the whole household: 'If a weaver has, as most have, a crop of flax, the wife and daughter spin it and he weaves it; if he is not a weaver but employed by his farm, they carry the yarn to market.'

During the eighteenth century Belfast became a major centre of the linen industry. At first the town was the commercial heart of the industry rather than a manufacturing centre. Merchants imported potash and oil of vitriol for bleaching and they soon acquired the bulk of the linen export trade. By the 1770s more than a fifth of the linen exported from Ireland was shipped from Belfast. The construction of the White Linen Hall in 1784, where drapers could market their finished cloth, was an indication of the importance of the linen trade to the growing town. According to the *Belfast News Letter* of 28 June 1785:

> *From the very large and complete assortment of linens at this market, and the attendance of so many of the principal English and Scottish buyers, we understand that both buyers and sellers agree in declaring that they now look upon our White Linen Market as certainly established ... Our quays at present and during the last week furnished a very agreeable spectacle; the ships for London, Chester, Liverpool, Whitehaven, Workington and Glasgow ranged in a line and gaily dressed with colours and streamers flying, taking in their cargoes of white linens sold in our Hall.*

John Barrow, who visited the town in the mid-1830s, was struck by the

> *verdant fields, intersected by bleaching-grounds covered with linen as white as snow, – afforded a cheerful and lively prospect, more particularly to a stranger not accustomed in his own country to look upon the latter object. The linen is laid out in long strips, the width of the web, and, with the blades of grass standing up between them, has the effect, from a little distance, which is produced just when the snow is in the act of dissolving with the warmth of the sun.*

The Green Linen Market, Donegall Street, Belfast. T M Baynes, Ireland, illustrated (1831).

In 1830 there were two linen mills in Belfast; by 1850 there were thirty-two with over half a million spindles and Belfast was well on its way to replacing Leeds and Dundee as the major linen manufacturer in the country. William Makepeace Thackeray wrote in 1840: 'A fine night-exhibition in the town is that of the huge spinning-mills which surround it, and of which the thousand windows are lighted up at nightfall, and may be seen from almost all quarters of the city.' Thackeray visited Mulholland's factory in York Street. Originally a cotton factory, it had burned down in 1828. It was replaced by a five-storey factory with three steam engines driving some 8,000 flax-spinning spindles. Thackeray was impressed by the scale of the operations:

> *There are nearly five hundred girls employed in it. They work in huge long chambers, lighted by numbers of windows, hot with steam, buzzing and humming with hundreds of thousands of whirling wheels, that all take their motion from a steam-engine which lives apart in a hot cast-iron temple of its own, from which it communicates with the innumerable machines that the five hundred girls preside over ... They work for twelve hours daily, in rooms of which the heat is intolerable to a stranger; but in spite of it they looked gay, stout, and healthy; nor were their forms much concealed by the very simple clothes they wear while in the mill.*

The spinning mills were built in green-field sites along the lower Falls and Shankill Roads. The mill owners built row upon row of terraced houses for their rapidly expanding workforce. These densely populated streets created the nucleus of west Belfast. In these houses close-knit communities developed, with each generation following its predecessor into the spinning mills and factories. These areas soon developed along sectarian lines as Catholic workers settled in the Falls Road area while Protestants gravitated towards the Shankill, Ballymacarrett and Ballynafeigh region.

Few attempts were made to reduce dangers to health in the mills and factories in Ireland until the twentieth century. Linen workers ran the risk of being maimed or killed by exposed machinery. Injury and death were endemic and frequent accounts of accidents appear in local news-papers. The *Belfast News Letter*, 1 May 1854, reported that an employee

Weaving factory. Hogg Collection, Ulster Museum.

of Messrs Rowan of York Street was not expected to recover: 'She was engaged at the carding part of the machinery and her hair by some means got entangled in the machinery in which the greater part of the scalp was removed from the head.'

Conditions were often primitive. In 1867 Dr John Moore writing on the influence of flax-spinning on the health of mill workers, was concerned about the spinning rooms where 'little girls are engaged, and here it is that the tender form of childhood is often in danger of being taxed beyond that it is able to bear'. Ten years later Dr C D Purdon drew attention to the damaging effect of flax dust on the lungs of mill workers. He found that their 'mortality from Phthisis, etc., is very high ... this affection of the lungs, that flax dressers suffer so much from, is so well known to the army surgeons that they have forbidden the recruiting sergeants to enlist any from this department'. In the case of machine boys, Dr Purdon found that dust was so dense that it quickly entered the lungs. 'In severe and well marked attacks', he concluded, 'the paroxysm of cough and dyspnoea lasts for a considerable time, and does not pass off

until the contents of the stomach are ejected, and often blood is spat up.'
He continued:

> *In a great number of instances the lad is obliged to leave the
> mill, and seek for employment in healthier trades. But still in cold
> weather he suffers from cough and shortness of breath, and in many
> cases his life is terminated by Phthisis ... numbers linger out a
> diseased existence, in other callings, only to terminate in death.*

Workers also suffered from exhaustion. Employers got around the
1847 Factory Act, limiting hours of work for women and children to ten a
day, by introducing a relay system. According to Dr Moore:

> *Those who have been long in the atmosphere of the spinning-room
> generally become pale and anaemic, and consequently pre-disposed
> to those ailments which spring from such a state of constitution.
> Children placed there early and compelled to keep upon their feet
> the entire day, as the nature of their employment obliges them to do
> often, suffer from the young and tender bones, which form the arch
> of the foot, being crushed and flattened.*

Thomas Gallaher's tobacco factory, York Street, Belfast, c.1900. Ulster Museum.

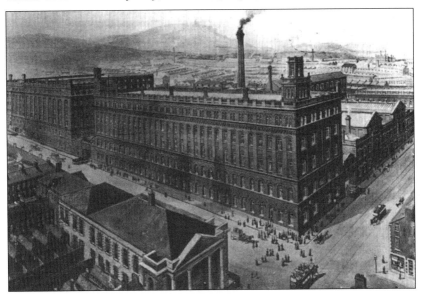

It was not until 1874 that hours were successfully cut down to ten every weekday and six on Saturdays, and even then employers added an extra duty of cleaning machines after hours. Until 1874 the usual working day began at 5 am and ended at 7 or 8 pm. Thereafter, until the beginning of the twentieth century, the working day began at 6.30 am and finished at 6 pm, with two three-quarter-hour breaks.

Childhood as we understand it today, as purely a time of play, of learning and amusement, was virtually non-existent for the majority of our Victorian ancestors. It was the preserve of the upper classes and the prosperous middles classes. Millions of children in the nineteenth century had the experience of working in a grown-up world by the time they were 10. Both boys and girls went out to work because of the overwhelming necessity to get every penny into the household. Children had, of course, worked since time immemorial, but the new mechanized age created working and living conditions that were shocking. Factories, now steam-powered and no longer dependent upon a steady water supply, moved into the towns and cities where there was a plentiful supply of child labour. Many factories were operated by apprentice pauper children from the nearby workhouses. They were housed in barrack-like 'prentice houses so that they could not for long escape the confines of the factory. Only marginally better off were the so-called 'free' children who still lived at home in the surrounding slums.

The minimum age for starting at the spinning mill or weaving factory was 8 years until 1874, when it was raised to 10 years, 11 years in 1891 and 12 years in 1901. These juveniles or 'half-timers' attended school either in the mornings or afternoons, or on alternate days. Dangerous machinery and a polluted atmosphere produced horrific injuries and often fatal illnesses. Many children ended up cripples. The law was openly flouted. As only four inspectors were appointed to monitor this legislation, factory owners would continue to employ very young children. 'The deadliest sin in the labour conditions of Ireland' declared Robert Lynd,

> *is neither the low wage paid to unskilled labourers nor that paid to women. It is the system under which boys and girls hardly out or their infancy are employed in the mills at a wage of 3s. 6d. a week. The child half-timer in Lancashire is often an object of sympathy. The plight of the Ulster half-timer, however, is infinitely more*

pitiable. In Lancashire the child really works half-time every day of the week and goes to school during the other part of the day. In Ulster the child works full time three days in the week, and attends school on the remaining days. The results which follow, when children of twelve years old or thereabouts are kept working for ten hours a day during three days in the week in a humid atmosphere of from 70 to 80 degrees Fahrenheit, might have been foreseen. Vitality is slowly squeezed out of them, and it is hardly an exaggeration to say that from the age of 15 upwards they die like flies.

Outside of the hazardous conditions in the factories, children were highly visible on the streets of Irish towns and cities. According to the report of the Inter-Departmental Committee of the Employment of Children during School Age, published in 1902, there were in Dublin 433 boys under 16 selling chiefly newspapers, and 144 girls selling newspapers, fruit or fish. In Belfast there were 1,240 boys and 45 girls and in Cork boys only numbering 114. Police returns showed that as a rule the lot of these children was a wretched one. The principal dangers were late hours in the street, truancy, insufficient clothing, entering licensed premises to sell their goods. They were guilty of 'obstructing, annoying, importuning passengers, begging, fighting with other children, playing football or games in the street, using bad language and smoking'.

Chimney sweeps, also known as 'climbing boys', were probably the most wretched group of charity children during the later part of the eighteenth and early nineteenth centuries. They were employed by chimney sweeps to climb up narrow chimney flues dragging the brushes of their masters. It was estimated that there were 200 children employed climbing chimneys in Dublin in 1798. Their plight came to public attention in 1816 when a Dublin master sweep was accused of cruelty to a boy in his employment. During his trial he was shown to have flogged the child and burnt him with coals. When the wounds festered the child was dipped in cold water and then lashed and burnt again: the child died shortly afterwards 'of a general mortification'. The sweep was sentenced to be publicly whipped and such was the crush of the crowd gathered to witness the spectacle, that eleven men, women and children were crushed to death when balustrades on the steps of the Royal Exchange collapsed. The outcome of these events was that a Sunday School society was established in Kellet's School, a Protestant charity school in Dorset Street, Dublin, to help chimney boys. A parish priest established a rival school in Bride Street for Catholic children.

Most women in towns filled less skilled, poorly paid occupations. In the mid-1830s women in the Cork City parish of Shandon sorted feathers, prepared offal for market and collected wash and grain from the city distillery to feed their pigs. Others sold old clothes, shoes, potatoes, vegetables and dairy products. In *An Account of Ireland, Statistical and Political*, published in 1812, Edward Edward Wakefield complained that

> *Women in Ireland are treated more like beasts of burden than*
> *rational beings, and although I never saw one yoked to a plough …*
> *I have seen them degraded in a manner disgraceful to the other sex,*
> *and shocking to humanity. In the country they are subjected to all*
> *the drudgery generally performed by men; setting potatoes, digging*
> *turf, and the performance of the most laborious occupations. I have*
> *often watched them with the utmost attention, but never heard a*
> *woman disobey the command of her husband, or repine at his orders.*

There were few areas of employment which middle-class women could enter. Teaching and governessing were two of the mainstays for those forced to support themselves. Shop work was also considered respectable work for young women. Shop assistants worked long hours, six days a week. Wages were not much better than that of factory workers, though shop assistants had to maintain a higher standard in appearance and dress. Office work also began to open up for women at the turn of the century. Women within offices had lower status than men and also became associated with the less well-paid areas of typing and book keeping.

Nineteenth-century Belfast offered more opportunities for women's work than many British cities, especially from the mid-century with the rapid expansion of the linen industry. As a result there were substantially more women in Belfast than men. In 1841 there were 38,000 females and 32,000 males; in 1901 the ratio was 188,000 to 162,000. Women worked in the linen industry, which in 1901 employed 24,000 females but only 7,000 males. Women were also found in large numbers in the clothing trades (11,000 compared with 4,000 males) and in domestic service, which employed almost 8,000 women and girls and provided 13 per cent of all female employment. Journalist Harriet Martineau, in her *Letters from Ireland*, published in 1852, wrote:

> *In Belfast, the warehouses we saw were more than half peopled with women, engaged about the linens and muslins. And at the flax-works, near the city, not only were women employed in the spreading and drying, but in the rolling, roughing, and finishing, which had always till now been done by men. The men had struck for wages; and their work was given to girls, at 8d. per day.*

Many women were employed by textile firms working from home for very low wages. Although they avoided the horrors of factory life, Dr Bailie, the Belfast Medical Superintendent Officer of Health was of the opinion that 'Home work has no attractions for the indolent sloven, so that the homes of out-workers represent a fairly high average of cleanliness'. James Haslam, writing in 1911, commented that the

> *Irish out-workers make a brave endeavour to form a bright contrast to their poverty by keeping themselves clean. That, perhaps, makes their struggle all the more pathetic. They work steadily and persistently for one penny per hour, and in some cases less than one penny!*

He talked to one old woman who embroidered handkerchiefs at the rate of sevenpence per dozen; she managed to finish a dozen in one day.

> *Her day began at five o'clock in the moirning to do the housework, and other domestic duties, then she laboured unto ten, eleven and twelve o'clock at night. 'But why', I asked her, 'do you slave day after day for such a miserable pittance'. 'Well, sor', she said, 'it pays the rint; an' I want, sor, to see Jimmy serve his time to a dacent thrade'. And in order that Jimmy might have a chance, this woman was stitching herself into the grave.*

Chapter 7

THE IRISH POOR LAW AND THE GREAT FAMINE

The level of poverty and destitution in Ireland was noted by visitors during the early nineteenth century. Mr and Mrs Hall, who visited Ireland on the eve of the Great Famine, found beggars in many different parts of rural Ireland. 'In the country, where passers-by are not numerous, the aged or bed ridden beggar is frequently placed in a sort of handbarrow and laid at morning by the roadside, and not unfrequently their business is conducted on the backs of donkeys, often drawn about by some neighbour's child.' The government attempted to deal with Ireland's pressing social problems by imposing the English poor law system in Ireland. The destitute poor, who were previously granted relief at parish level, were to be accommodated in new workhouses where conditions were to be as unpleasant as was consistent with health.

By the 1840s Ireland had over 8,000,000 inhabitants, of whom more than four-fifths lived on the land. About half of this population depended for its subsistence on the potato. No one knows for certain when the potato arrived in Ireland although tradition has it that Sir Walter Raleigh brought them to the country. By the 1640s and 1650s potatoes were being grown as a garden crop throughout Ireland because they were well suited to the cool climate and wet soils. By the early nineteenth century over 2 million acres of land were under potatoes and they played a vital role in

Destitution in Ireland. Pictorial Times *(1846).*

the Irish economy. The potato enabled farmers to offer a patch of ground to any agricultural labourers he employed instead of money. The cotters, who rented a cabin and between one and one and a half acres of land upon which to grow potatoes, oats and possibly some flax, also depended for their survival on their potato patch. In the south and west it enabled fathers to subdivide their holdings to provide for sons and landless men to reclaim the mountain and the bog. The survival of these people depended on a good crop each season, for the potato could not be stored to relieve periods of scarcity like grain. Disaster when it came would be more sudden and complete than anyone could have imagined.

In 1833 the government appointed a commission under the chairmanship of Richard Whately, Archbishop of Dublin, to examine the level of poverty in Ireland. The commission's report found that there were 2,385,000 persons in want or distressed during thirty weeks of the year. To tackle the problem of poverty the government passed the Irish Poor Law Act in 1838 which established workhouses. The country was divided into 137 unions which were centred around market towns where a workhouse or union house was built with an infirmary and fever hospital attached. The boards of guardians were instructed to discourage all but the neediest paupers from applying to the workhouse from assistance. In their Sixth Annual Report, the Poor Law Commissioners admitted that it was no easy task to make conditions in the workhouse sufficiently bleak that it would deter only the most destitute:

> *It must be obvious to anyone conversant with the habits and mode of living of the Irish people that to establish a dietary in the work-house inferior to the ordinary diet of the poor classes would be difficult, if not, in many cases, impossible; and hence it has been contended that the workhouse system of relief is inapplicable to Ireland.*

The authorities were forced to rely on the 'regularity, order, strict enforcement of cleanliness, constant occupation, the preservation of decency and decorum, and exclusion of all the irregular habits and tempting excitements of life' to deter only the most desperate from seeking refuge within the workhouse. The Commissioners would later concede in their report for May 1848 that this had worked only too well.

> *If there has been anything unsatisfactory in the operation of the workhouse as a condition of relief in the present season of severe distress, it is, that in localities where destitution has undoubtedly prevailed, the unwillingness of some poor persons to avail themselves of this mode of relief has been so great, that they have sacrificed their own lives, or the lives of their children, by postponing acceptance too long, or by refusing such relief altogether.*

The management of the workhouses was the responsibility of the boards of guardians composed of elected representatives of the ratepayers in each union, together with ex-officio members including Justices of the Peace. While the guardians were legally responsible for the management of the workhouse and the collection and expenditure of money, the day-to-day running of the workhouse was carried out by a number of salaried officials. The staff consisted of a master, matron, clerk, chaplain, school-master, medical officer, porter and additional assistants and servants that the guardians deemed necessary. In terms of the management of the workhouse, the most important figure was the master. The sixth Annual

Report of the Poor Law Commissioners spelt out the twenty-four duties of the master. These included

> *reading prayers to the paupers before breakfast and after supper*
> *every day ... at which all paupers must attend; providing and*
> *enforcing the employment of the able-bodied paupers; training the*
> *youth and keeping the partially disabled paupers occupied to the*
> *extent of their ability; and to allow none who are capable of*
> *employment to be idle at any time.*

In an attempt to prevent the religious issue dominating the administration of the Irish Poor Law no person in holy orders or a regular minister of any religious denomination could serve on the boards of guardians. Section 48 of the Irish Poor Relief Act specified that each workhouse should have 'one fit person' appointed chaplain to the workhouse 'being in Holy Orders and of the Established Church, one other fit person being a Protestant Dissenter and one other fit person being a Priest or Clergyman of the Roman Catholic Church'. Chaplains were to celebrate divine service and to preach to the paupers every Sunday', they were to 'examine and catechise the children at least every month', and to record in a special book the progress of the children as well as the dates of their attendance at the workhouse. The clergy in many workhouses regarded each other with considerable hostility and a constant watch was kept to ensure that members of their flock were not poached by their opposite number.

The new workhouse-building project began in January 1839 with the arrival in Dublin of architect George Wilkinson. He had already designed a number of workhouses in England and Wales, including those at Thame, Stroud and Chipping Norton. The same design was used for all of the new workhouses. His brief from the Poor Law Commissioners stated that: 'The style of building is intended to be of the cheapest description compatible with durability; and effect is aimed at by harmony of proportion and simplicity of arrangement, all mere decoration being studiously excluded.' Workhouse construction proceeded with amazing speed, and by April 1843 Wilkinson was able to report that 112 of the new workhouses were finished, and 18 others were almost complete. Difficulties in collecting the poor rate, together with people's general reluctance to enter these forbidding structures, meant that, even by the summer of 1846, the workhouses were still only half-full. Dunfanaghy workhouse in County Donegal, for example, contained only five inmates. This situation changed dramatically as the catastrophe of the Great Famine hit Ireland.

The first sign of the potato blight occurred in Wexford and Waterford in September 1845 and then spread rapidly until about half the country was affected. On 18 October 1845 the *Illustrated London News* reported that:

> *Accounts received from different parts of Ireland show that the disease in the potato crops is extending far and wide, and causing great alarm amongst the peasantry. Letters from resident landlords feelingly describe the misery and consternation of the poor people around them, and earnestly urge the imperative necessity of speedy intervention on the part of the Government to ascertain the actual extent of the calamity, and provide wholesome food as a substitute for the deficient supply of potatoes.*

More than one-third of the crop was lost in 1845. In November, Prime Minister Sir Robert Peel spent £100,000 on Indian corn and meal in order to prevent soaring food prices in Ireland. In order to meet the growing distress, Peel established a relief commission and the formation of local committees was encouraged. Local voluntary contributions were supplemented, usually to the extent of two-thirds, by government grants. Relief works, with the government paying half the cost, were also set up to provide employment, for it was proposed to sell food rather than give it away. By the beginning of 1846 the *Belfast New Letter* was convinced that the worst was over. The newspaper rejected talk of widespread famine. 'It is quite true that in some of our districts extreme scarcity prevails, as is invariably the case at this season; but the most active ingenuity of the famine-mongers has failed to magnify that scarcity into a greater than ordinary calamity.'

The new Whig government, which took office in June 1846, also rejected talk of famine. The Prime Minister Lord John Russell was committed to laissez-faire, and believed it was wrong for the government to meddle in economic laws. He was convinced that the horror stories from Ireland were exaggerated. 'It must be thoroughly understood', he declared, 'that we cannot feed the people'. The driving force in the new government's response to the famine was that of Sir Charles Trevelyan, Assistant Secretary to the Treasury. He was determined to ensure that state intervention would not undermine the principle that the government's purpose was to help local effort, not to supplant it.

The potato crop had failed before and people hoped that the next harvest would be all right. However, the blight returned in 1846 and this time the failure was complete. The speed with which the blight struck added to the horror. The Revd Samuel Montgomery, rector of Ballinascreen in County Londonderry, wrote an account in his parish register:

> *On the last days of July and the first six days of August 1846 the potatoes were suddenly attacked, when in their full growth, with a sudden blight. The tops were first observed to wither and then, on looking to the roots, the tubers were found hastening to Decomposition. The entire crop that in the Month of July appeared so luxuriant, about the 15th August manifested only blackened and withered stems. The whole atmosphere in the Month of September was tainted with the odour of the decaying potatoes.*

In December 1846, a local magistrate in west Cork visited Skibbereen with bread to feed the starving population. Nothing prepared him for the horrors he witnessed. In the first hovel he entered he found 'six famished and ghastly skeletons, to all appearances dead' huddled in a corner on some filthy straw. He was soon surrounded by more than two hundred destitute and hungry people 'such phantoms, such frightful spectres as no words can describe, either from famine or from fever. Their demoniac yells are still ringing in my ears, and their horrible images are fixed upon my brain.'

The Whig government resolved that there would be no government buying, the supply of food was to be left exclusively to private enterprise. Relief was limited to public works and this time the government insisted the cost be borne entirely by the rates, that is, by the Irish landlords. Meanwhile winter set in, the harshest and longest in living memory. Hungry mobs roamed the county but above all they poured into the relief works. The numbers employed leapt from 30,000 in September to half a million in December. Horrors stories began to emerge of the suffering of the Irish peasantry. A Special Reporter for *The Cork Examiner* visited Skibbereen in December 1846 and was appalled by what he saw:

> *dead bodies of children flung into holes hastily scratched in the earth, without a shroud or coffin – wives travelling ten miles to beg the charity of a coffin for a dead husband, and bearing it back that weary distance – a Government official offering the one-tenth of a sufficient supply of food at famine prices – every field becoming a grave, and the land a wilderness!*

The situation reached its worst by February 1847 when great gales blew and the ground was blanketed in thick snow. A fever epidemic spread throughout the country. What people call 'Famine Fever' was in fact two separate diseases, typhus and relapsing fever. Other diseases such as scurvy spread, particularly among those forced to depend on Indian meal which is lacking in vitamin C. The fear of infection caused people to refuse food and shelter to even their near neighbours. Fear of contracting fever through contact with the bodies of the dead (caused by the transfer of lice, though this was not known at the time) caused people to discontinue traditional burial ceremonies. Bodies lay for days in cabins which the survivors had deserted. Many others lay were found on the roadside, often with no means of identification.

Funeral at Skibbereen. Illustrated London News *(1847).*

By the beginning of 1847 the Cabinet at last began to realize that a radical change of policy was needed. A temporary Act was passed in February 1847, to establish soup kitchens to help bridge the gap until the harvest of the following autumn. Soup kitchens had been used for relief of distress on previous occasions in both Ireland and Britain from the middle of eighteenth century. The provision and distribution of food was to be a charge on the local rates, though the government would where necessary, advance funds to start the new scheme. Alexis Soyer, the famous chef of the London Reform Club, was sent to Ireland to set up a model soup kitchen where soup could be made according to the same recipe as that which he had devised for the London poor. Soyer's soup recipes required little or no meat. For this reason he claimed that a quart of nutritious soup could be made for 3/4d. Critics declared that it was not so much 'soup for the poor' as 'poor soup'.

By July 1847 the number of people being fed each day reached three million. Starving people were forced to stand in orderly lines with cans or

Soup House. Illustrated London News *(1847).*

bowls in their hands. For many in the south and west of Ireland it came down to a choice between starvation or emigration. The poor cotters and the small farmers left the country in great numbers. Liverpool was the first city to be invaded. By June 1847 it was estimated that over 300,000 destitute Irish people had landed in the town. Many sailed on to North America and Canada.

The blight was not as severe during the autumn of 1847, bringing with it a glimmer of hope. The spring of 1848, however, was very cold, with heavy falls of snow. Many poor people believed that the frost would kill the blight and planted potatoes paid for by what little money they had left. However, the blight returned with greater force than before. With so many people unable to pay their rent, some landlords evicted tenants from their estates. As soon as they were forced out, their houses were levelled to prevent them from returning. Some of those who were evicted found shelter in the cabins of friends or relatives. Sometimes they built makeshift homes called scalps or scalpeens in the ruins of their old cabins or in ditches or wasteland. Throughout Ireland more than 48,000 families were evicted between 1849 and 1854, amounting to a total of almost a

Ejectment. Illustrated London News *(1848).*

quarter of a million people. Captain Arthur Kennedy reported that: 'they exist like animals till starvation or the inclemency of the weather drives them to the workhouse'.

The workhouses could not cope with the large numbers of destitute and starving people who needed help. When they were built they were expected to house between 80,000 and 100,000 people. In their Annual Report dated 1 May 1848, the Irish Poor Law Commissioners commented that

> *in the workhouses, we may state that more than 800,000 persons are daily relieved at the charge of the poor-rates, consisting chiefly of the most helpless part of the most indigent classes in Ireland; and we cannot doubt that of this number a very large proportion are by this means, and this means alone, daily preserved from death through want of food.*

Nevertheless, many preferred to die than enter the workhouse. The death rate in Lurgan workhouse was so appalling that at the end of January 1847 the Poor Law Commissioners demanded an explanation. Dr Bell, the medical officer, wrote in reply:

> *Many diseases are now prevalent in the country, and the great majority of new admissions are, when brought into the house, at the point of death, in a moribund state. Many have been known to die on the road, and others on being raised from their beds to come to the workhouse have died before they could be put into the cart, and numbers have died in less than 24 hours subsequent to their admission ... many dying persons are sent for admission merely that coffins many be obtained for them at the expense of the Union.*

In June 1847 the government's determination that relief would only be granted to those who entered the workhouse crumbled in the face of the overwhelming disaster. The Poor Law Amendment Act authorized the granting of outdoor assistance even to the able-bodied and according to the Commissioners 'the entire number of persons provided with daily sustenance in Ireland, may be stated, in round numbers, to be 1,000,000, or about one eighth part of the whole population'.

Famine conditions continued in much of the west of Ireland until 1850. By 1851 the population was six and a half million, two million less than the estimated population of 1845, a million having emigrated and another million dead as a result of starvation and disease. In the workhouse the number of inmates began to fall. Harriet Martineau contrasted the inmates in Irish workhouses in 1852 with those in England. In England

> *men and women have either begun life at a disadvantage, or have failed in life through some incapacity, physical or moral; or they are the children of such that we find in the workhouses; and we expect therefore to see a deteriorated generation – sickly or stupid, or in some way ill-conditioned. In Irish workhouses it is not this sort of people that are to be found. Indeed, the one thing heard about them in England is that they are ready to die rather than enter the workhouse. They are the victims of a sudden, sweeping calamity, which bore no relation to vice, folly, laziness, or improvidence. In the first season of famine, the inmates were a pretty fair specimen of the inhabitants at large; and they are now the strongest and best-conditioned of those original inmates. They are now the people who lived through the famine which carried off the weak and sickly.*

Harriet Martineau, visiting Ballyvaughan workhouse in 1852, found during harvest-time only twenty able-bodied male inmates, and these were suffering from some ailment or infirmity. Of the 667 inmates, 300 were children.

> *That was a fact only too easily understood: they were orphaned by the famine. There were many widows and 'deserted women'; the 'desertion' being that their husbands had gone to England to work, leaving their families to the union. The expectation was that most of these men would come back, with more or less money. Some would probably go from Liverpool to America, leaving their families where they were till they could send funds to carry them out to the United States.*

The poor law system worked best between the 1850s and 1870s when the numbers receiving outdoor relief was small compared with those provided for in the workhouse. During this period, the Boards of Guardians played an increasingly important role in the administration of local government. In 1872, the Boards of Guardians came under the control of the Local Government Board which became one of the most important departments of the Irish administration. To its original functions of supervising the poor law and the dispensary system, the government added many others, including responsibility for public health. From 1856 Boards of Guardians acted as burial boards and from 1865 as sewer authorities for those areas of the counties which were outside the responsibility of the town commissioners. The guardians' powers were further increased by the Public Health Acts of 1874 and 1878 which made the poor law boards rural sanitary authorities giving them power to destroy unsound food, supervise slaughter-houses and deal with infectious diseases in hospitals. The guardians later were made responsible for the supervision of the hospitals set up under the Tuberculosis Prevention (Ireland) Act of 1908 and the board also became the central authority under the Old Age Pensions Act of 1908.

By this time the function of the workhouse had gradually changed. It became an institution for the old, sick and vagrants. Additional powers were given to the Boards of Guardians under the Act of 1862. This Act declared that it was 'expedient to extend to cases of sickness or accident the powers which the guardians now possess, in regard to fever cases'. This was a very important development as it opened the workhouse hospitals to sick people who were not destitute.

After the partition of Ireland in 1921, many of the remaining workhouses became county homes for the aged, others were converted into district or fever hospitals, a few became county hospitals and the rest were closed. The old Boards of Guardians were replaced by Boards of Health (later Boards of Health and Public Assistance) and a new system of Home Assistance replaced the old workhouse relief. It was a similar story in Northern Ireland where many workhouses became district hospitals during the 1920s and 1930s, although the poor law itself survived until 1946. For the older generation, however, the shadow of the workhouse remained and elderly people were bitterly afraid to enter their local hospitals where so many of their contemporaries had lived and died as inmates.

Chapter 8

MIGRATION

The Irish were by far the most important migrant group in Britain during the nineteenth century. They made their way to London and to all of the growing industrial towns of the Midlands, the north of England, and the central lowlands of Scotland. Victorian writers associated them with poverty, crime, drunkenness and Catholicism, which helped create the stereotype of the stage Irishman. Thomas Carlyle wrote in *Chartism*, in 1840:

> *England is guilty towards Ireland; and reaps at last, in full measure, the fruit of fifteen generations of wrong-doing ... Crowds of miserable Irish darken our towns ... The uncivilised Irishman, not by his strength, but by the opposite of strength, drives out the Saxon native, takes possession in his room. There abides he, in his squalor and unreason, in his falsity and drunken violence, as the ready-made nucleus of degradation and disorder.*

However, many prospered in their adoptive country and some like Richard Brindley Sheridan, Oliver Goldsmith, Edmund Burke and George Bernard Shaw scaled the heights of English society.

Irish migration to Britain was not a purely nineteenth-century phenomenon but dates back to ancient times. From the sixth century AD the Scotti or Scots, a warlike Celtic race from Northern Ireland, extended their north-eastern kingdom of Dalriada into what is now Argyll, Kintyre and the neighbouring islands. Close links were also forged between the south-east of Ireland and Wales during the early medieval period. The north-western part of Wales was temporarily ruled over by Laigin, people from Leinster, until they were driven out by the British King Cunedda in the fifth century. A reminder of the people of Leinster is preserved in the name of the peninsula, Lleyn, in Gwynedd.

The migration between Ireland and Britain during the Norman period was mostly the other way. Anglo-Norman armies invaded Ireland during the later half of the twelfth century and established colonies in various parts of the country and this marked the beginning of large-scale migration from Wales and England. The Irish presence in Britain from the Middle Ages is indicated by surnames such as le Yreys, Irlond, Hibernia and Iryssh. Both the 1332 lay subsidy returns for Lancashire and the 1379 poll tax returns for Liverpool include the name de Irlond and the surname Ireland is still most commonly found in this area. The poverty of many of these early Irish migrants can be judged in the repeated attempts by the authorities to force them to return to Ireland. In 1243 a statute was invoked for the expulsion of Irish beggars and again in 1413. An Act of 1572 provided for their repatriation to Ireland at the cost of the county which first received them. A royal proclamation of the late 1680s complained that 'in and about the city of London, and in parts in and about Her Majesty's court ... there did haunt and repair a great multitude of wandering persons, many of whom were men from Ireland'.

Legislation did not prevent the Irish seeking refuge in England during times of famine or wars in Ireland. During the last years of Elizabeth I a long and bloody war of subjugation was fought in Ireland and many Irish refugees fled to England by way of Bristol. The Plantation of Ulster during the early seventeenth century also produced a backwash of migration to England. London was a favourite destination for Irish settlers from the sixteenth century. According to contemporary sources there was a colony of Irish sailors and merchants by the Thames, Irish lawyers at the Inns of Court, and writers and dramatists in Whitefriars and Alsatia by the beginning of the seventeenth century. In St Giles especially there was a colony of 'unskilled labourers, builders' labourers, chairmen, porters, coal-heavers, milk-sellers and street hawkers, publicans and lodging-house keepers, apparently chiefly catering for their own countrymen'.

Covent Garden Labourers, many were 'Seven Dials Irish'. From John Thomson, Victorian London Street Life *(originally publ. 1877).*

The emergence of the northern towns as great commercial and industrial centres during the eighteenth century encouraged an influx of Irish settlers. The Irish flocked to Britain during the harvesting period and followed the harvests round – haymaking in June, turnip-hoeing in July, corn-harvesting in August, hop-picking or fruit-picking in September. The Irish reaper was already a familiar figure in the summer landscape of eighteenth-century England, and by about 1834, it seems from the poor inquiry's parish survey that some 40,000 reapers were migrating annually to Britain. Politician William Cobbett described these seasonal workers as 'squalid creatures ... with rags hardly sufficient to hide the nakedness of their bodies'.

In spite of the steady haemorrhaging of its population, Ireland on the eve of the Great Famine had over 8,000,000 inhabitants. More than four-fifths lived on the land and about half of this population depended for its subsistence on the potato. The eighteenth-century economist Adam Smith, commenting on the Irish in London, attributed their health and handsome looks to the potato:

> *The Chairman, porters, coalheavers in London, and those un-*
> *fortunate women who live by prostitution, the strongest men and*
> *the most beautiful women perhaps in the British dominions, are said*
> *to be, the greater part of them, from the lowest rank of people in*
> *Ireland, who are generally fed from this root. No food can afford a*
> *more decisive proof of its nourishing quality, or its being particularly*
> *suitable to the health of the human constitution.*

During the late 1840s the potato crop failed over the whole country, and that failure was repeated in successive years. Many starving and destitute people fled to the industrial towns on the British mainland. Liverpool was the first city to be invaded. At the beginning of 1847 *The Times* warned that 'the anticipated invasion of Irish pauperism had commenced, 15,000 have already, within the last three months, landed in Liverpool and block up her thoroughfare with masses of misery'. By June, it was estimated that 300,000 destitute Irish people had landed in the town. *The Times* predicted that 'in a few years more a Celtic Irishman will be as rare in Connemara as is the Red Indian on the shores of Manhattan'.

In spite of their rural background the vast majority of Irish migrants settled in towns. In both 1851 and 1861 at least thirty-one towns in England and Wales had a recorded Irish-born population of over 1,000. Some of the towns are not normally associated with an Irish presence: Bath, Colchester, Derby, Newport, Plymouth, Portsmouth and Southampton.

By 1852, 22 per cent of Liverpool's population and 13 per cent of Manchester's was Irish-born. The largest settlement occurred in London, which according to the 1851 census was home to 108,548 Irish-born settlers. Today, more than 150 years after the Famine, the districts settled at that time are still identified as Irish: Hammersmith, Camden Town, Paddington and Islington.

The Irish were often accused of working for lower rates of pay and thereby depressing wage levels. They were seen as strike-breakers who would gladly work for lower wages. The idea that the Irish were undercutting wages often led to violent reprisals. In 1736, for example, English weavers rioted against Irish workers who allegedly undercut the going rate. In 1826 violence erupted at the Bute ironworks in the Rhymney Valley when the news spread that cheap gangs of Irish labour were being employed to build new blast furnaces. During the construction of the Caledonian and Union canals in Scotland there were numerous clashes between Irish and Scottish workers.

Long-term residency in Britain did not prevent local authorities from sending back to Ireland families who had fallen on hard times. Irish newspapers are littered with heart-rending stories of destitute families bundled

Irish navvies building Britain's railways. From the National Railway Museum Pictorial Collection.

back to Ireland by local authorities in England and Scotland. The *Irish Times* for 4 January 1860 reported:

> *Sarah Miller, fifty years of age, a native of Belfast, was sent here by the authorities of Newcastle-on-Tyne. She was thirty years in England and Scotland. She was sent to the Union Workhouse, after receiving the necessary attention. Mary Hopkins, twenty-three years of age, and her infant child, were sent here by the authorities of Newcastle-on-Tyne. The poor woman is a native of Mayo, and has been twelve years in England. They were put to lodgings for one night, and then sent to the workhouses, where they remained for five nights. Captain McBride kept them at lodgings for ten nights, and then sent them to Sligo, on the way to where the woman belongs. On the 14th December, Patrick Conway, a poor cripple, was landed from the Glasgow steamer, without money or friends. Captain McBride gave him refreshment, and sent him to the Union Hospital, and when he recovers will send him home to Newry.*

Victorian writers frequently portrayed the Irish as living in ghettos, known as 'Little Irelands' which became a nucleus of disease, poverty, alcoholism and crime. Friedrick Engels, in his depiction of Irish immigrants living in the slums of Manchester, helped shape this image:

> *Here lie two groups of about two hundred cottages, most of which are built on the back-to-back principle. Some four thousand people, mostly Irish, inhabit this slum ... The creatures who inhabit these dwellings and even their dark, wet cellars, and who live confined amidst all this filth and foul air – which cannot be dissipated because of the surrounding lofty buildings – must surely have sunk to the lowest level of humanity.*

In reality the Irish in Britain were a diverse group and a significant minority of them were middle-class who blended more easily into British society. In cities such as Bristol there was no Irish quarter and the Irish were well distributed throughout the city and spanned the whole range of social groups. In Liverpool, although Exchange, Vauxhall and Scotland wards were recognized as Irish districts, their population was rarely more than 50 per cent Irish. Even within Irish communities there was considerable diversity; both Connacht men and Orangemen from Ulster were looked down upon by their fellow countrymen and religious differences were a frequent source of conflict between Irishmen in Britain.

Northerners tended to travel from Derry to Glasgow and then to southern Scotland; Munster people from Cork to Bristol and then to London and southern England. In 1834, Bishop Scott of Glasgow remarked that 'almost all the Irish in this city and neighbourhood come here from the northern counties of Ireland', a fact confirmed by studies of Dundee, Paisley and Greenock. Two-thirds of the London Irish in 1861–71 were born in 'western Munster', though a well-placed Liverpool witness claimed in 1834 that more Irish was spoken in London than Liverpool because immigrants from Connacht habitually passed on to London. Nevertheless, for most Connacht emigrants Dublin was the most convenient port of embarkation, while Liverpool was the closest major British port to Dublin. Studies of census schedules for various Yorkshire towns between 1851 and 1871 indicate disproportionately high rates of emigration from counties such as Mayo and Sligo. In Leeds about one Irish settler in seven came from these counties, in Bradford over one in four, in York up to one in two. Connacht people also dominated Irish movement to Staffordshire towns such as Wolverhampton and Wednesbury.

The influx of Irish immigrants ensured that by the mid-Victorian period Roman Catholicism was the growing denomination in Britain. From time to time rabid anti-Catholicism exploded into violence. The most famous eighteenth-century manifestation was the anti-Catholic Gordon Riots of 1780. In June of that year the eccentric Lord George Gordon, head of a Protestant Association committed to the repeal of the Roman Catholic Relief Act of 1778, was escorted by a group of his London supporters when he presented a petition to Parliament. Rioting followed and houses, chapels and distilleries were sacked. Martial law was declared and order was only restored by regular troops and the militia.

The Stockport Riots of 1852 were partly prompted by the re-establishment from Rome of the Catholic hierarchy in Britain in 1850. The government reacted by passing the Ecclesiastical Titles Bill which forbade the carrying of Catholic insignia and banners in public places. The Irish in Stockport had risen from 300 at the beginning of the century to over 8,000 by 1852. Their annual procession in June 1852 came only days after the royal proclamation of the Ecclesiastical Titles Bill. The procession passed off peacefully but on the following day trouble broke out between rival parties. The rioting lasted spasmodically for three days before it was finally put down by the combined efforts of the police and hundreds of special constables. Sixty-seven people were seriously wounded; one was killed and some died later of wounds. Many Irish families fled to the surrounding countryside.

Throughout the late 1860s the Irish Protestant polemicist William Murphy staged a series of anti-Catholic meetings in English towns. During a meeting in Birmingham in June 1867 he told a gathering of 3,000 people that the Pope was a 'rag and bone picker'. The meeting was attacked by a number of Irish labourers and serious rioting followed, the unrest lasting for several days. Similar outbreaks of violence occurred throughout the winter of 1867 as Murphy travelled around the Midlands, speaking at Stafford, Walsall and other small towns. Similar events took place the following year and in May 1868 a Protestant mob ransacked the Irish sectors of Ashton-under-Lyme, demolishing two chapels, a school and over 100 houses and shops.

This sequence of events was brought to an end in Whitehaven, in April 1871. Murphy was scheduled to give a series of lectures but in a pre-emptive strike, 200–300 Irish miners from the nearby pit village of Cleator Moor invaded the town, trapped Murphy in the Oddfellows' Hall and threw him down the stairs. Murphy died a year later but his death was attributed to the injuries he had received in Whitehaven. In Cumberland the death of 'Martyr Murphy' resulted in a resurgence of Orangeism and the north-east of England in the 1870s and 1880s witnessed numerous outbreaks of street disorder, especially on the 'Glorious Twelfth' of July when Orangemen celebrated the Williamite victory at the battle of the Boyne.

Unfortunately census records do not distinguish Irish immigrants by religion and Protestant numbers can only be calculated by subtracting, where they can be identified, the number of Catholics from figures for the Irish as a whole. The census of Glasgow in 1831 made by James Cleland, for example, revealed 35,554 Irish out of a total population of 202,426, but only 19,333 were listed as Catholics. It has been estimated that a quarter of Irish immigrants to Scotland during the nineteenth century were Protestant. The first Orange lodge set up in Scotland was in the weaving town of Maybole about 1800 and by 1835 twelve lodges had been established in Glasgow. By the 1850s Ulster Protestants established specifically Protestant areas such as Govan where they would later become closely identified with Glasgow Rangers Football Club. Meanwhile clubs like Celtic and Hibernian maintained close links with the Irish Catholic community in Glasgow and Edinburgh. Until well into the twentieth century matches between the Glasgow rivals would often explode into sectarian violence.

Over the centuries many Irishmen and women would make a major contribution to the political and cultural life of their adopted country. Oliver Goldsmith, Bernard Shaw, C S Lewis and Louis McNeice are just of the few Irish-born writers and dramatists who made a major contribution to English literature. Some, like Edmund Burke or Richard Brindley Sheridan, were successful as writers and as politicians. Elizabeth Farren, Countess of Derby, took a more unconventional path to success. Born in County Cork in 1759, her father was a surgeon and apothecary who died early, probably from drink. His widow was forced to take to the stage in the English provinces in order to support herself and her children. Elizabeth made her first appearance in London in 1777 as Miss Hardcastle in *She Stoops to Conquer*. Her natural elegance wit and charm made her popular in London society and she married Lord Derby on 1 May 1797, six weeks after the death of his first wife.

The flow of emigration from Ireland continued for much of the twentieth century. From the First World War Britain replaced the United States as the first choice destination, a position that it holds

Oscar Wilde an Irish migrant who made good in his adopted country.

to the present day. Irish migration to Britain surged during the Second World War and after as the Irish economy stagnated and British industry expanded; about half a million people left the Irish Republic during the 1950s alone. Today more Irish people live in London than anywhere else in the world except Dublin and Belfast. The Irish in Britain have never become a distinct and unified community, yet nor have they been fully integrated into British life. They still occupy, in the words of the Irish Liverpool MP, T P O'Connor, during the First World War, a 'curious middle place'.

Chapter 9

EMIGRATION

For much of the eighteenth and nineteenth century it seemed as if the most energetic part of the Irish population had either left or were constantly leaving the country. In the course of the eighteenth century many of the Presbyterians of the North, irritated by the Test Act and suffering from restrictions on the woollen trade or periodical depressions in the linen industry, emigrated to the English colonies in America. There was always a steady trickle of Catholic Irish who joined the English Army or Navy and a regular exodus of labourers into England, and this became a mass exodus in the decade during and after the Great Famine when more than two million people were to emigrate – more than in the preceding two and a half centuries.

In the summer of 1718 James McGregor, dissenting minister of the Aghadowey congregation in Co. Londonderry, announced to his congregation in the meeting-house the first mass emigration of Scots-Irish to the New World:

> *Brethren, let us depart for God has appointed a new country for us to dwell in. It is called New England. Let us be free of these Pharaohs, these rackers of rents and screwers of tithes and let us go into the land of Canaan. We are the Lord's ain people and he shall divide the ocean before us.*

Five ships left Derry quay for Boston where McGregor got a grant of land on the frontier of the Merrimac river in New Hampshire, which he

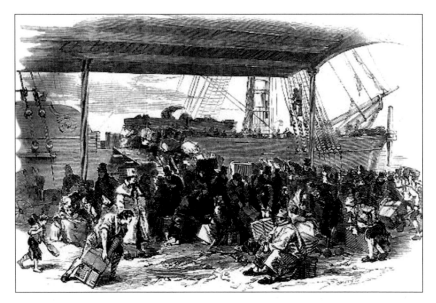

Embarkation. Illustrated London News *(1850).*

named Londonderry in honour, he said, of Ulster Protestants' 'finest hour'. Londonderry spawned a group of Ulster settlements in southern New Hampshire with names like Antrim and Hillsborough.

The Revd McGregor was not taking them into the unknown. There had long been extensive trade between Ireland and America, with Irish linen and provisions being exchanged for American flaxseed, flour and tobacco. In the last decades of the seventeenth century there had been a steady trickle of emigrants from Ulster to Maryland and the area close to Philadelphia. More important for encouraging fresh emigration was the presence of Presbyterian ministers from Ulster in the Middle Colonies. The most famous of these was Francis Makemie, who came from Co. Donegal to Maryland in the 1680s and is now regarded as the Founding Father of American Presbyterianism.

The first wave of emigration was enough to bring about a change in the law. In 1719 an Act was passed to permit Dissenters to celebrate their own form of worship. The numbers leaving the country continued to rise nevertheless and between 1725 and 1727 it has been estimated that 3,500 left Ulster. Primate Boulter informed the Duke of Newcastle in

November 1728 that: 'The humour has spread like a contagious distemper, and the people will hardly hear any body that tries to cure them of their madness. The worst is that it affects only protestants, and reigns chiefly in the north, which is the seat of our linen manufacture.'

During the seventeenth century landlords had sought to attract Protestant tenants with long leases at low rents. By the early part of the eighteenth century these leases began to expire and rents rose sharply due to the demand for land. Repeated harvest failures made it impossible for many to pay their rents. Tenants were therefore tempted to sell their interest in their holdings (a right accepted by most landlords and later known as the Ulster Custom) to raise the capital for their tickets to America. Sometimes an enterprising landlord would encourage his tenants to emigrate. Arthur Dobbs from Carrickfergus in Co. Antrim purchased with Colonel John Selwyn 400,000 acres of land in the south-east of North Carolina in 1745. He was active in seeking out settlers for his land – even offering to pay their passage money – because the terms of his grant laid down that any land on which fewer than one white settler for every 200 acres had been planted by 1755 would revert to the Crown.

The main attraction of the American colonies was for those who were eager to improve their prospects – younger sons in particular. The earliest Ulster letter relating to emigration, which is deposited in PRONI, dates from 1758, and was written by David Lindsey to his cousin Thomas Fleming in Pennsylvania. The letter illustrates the attraction of cheap

Emigrants. Illustrated London News *(1851)*.

land across the Atlantic and the pressure on the land system at home. Lindsey writes 'The good bargains of your lands in that country doe greatly encourage me to pluck up my spirits and make redie for the journey, for we are now oppressed with our lands at 8s. per acre and other improvements, cutting our land in two-acre parts and quicking, and only two years time for doing it all – yea, we cannot stand more.'

During the early part of the eighteenth century, many of these emigrants could not afford the passage money and had to work their way out by various means. However, as the century wore on there was a marked rise in the affluence and social status of the average emigrant. As a general rule it is fair to say that the bulk of those who emigrated to America before the War of Independence were forced by their poverty to become indentured servants. This meant that the emigrant signed an indenture to serve the master of a ship or his assignees for an agreed period. On landing in America, the indenture would be sold by the master to the highest bidder. When the emigrants arrived advertisements were inserted in the American newspapers. For example, the people of Charleston were informed in 1734: 'Just imported and to be sold . . . Irish servants, men and women, of good trades, from the north of Ireland, Irish linen, household furniture, butter, cheese, chinaware and all sorts of dry goods . . .' One army officer, in a letter to his father in Lisburn after he had seen the arrival at Philadelphia of servants from the north of Ireland, commented that 'They sell the servants here as they do their horses, and advertise them as they do their oatmeal and beef.'

The most emigrant port was Londonderry, though Belfast was never far behind, with Newry, Sligo, Larne and Killybegs following in that order. Until about 1800 the great majority of emigrant ships took their passengers to the Delaware ports of Philadelphia, Newcastle and Wilmington, but New York became steadily more important and there was always a sizeable movement to Baltimore and Charleston. The ships were primarily designed for cargo, and below decks only children could stand upright. The *William*, which sailed from Newry to Boston in 1766, had a height of four feet nine inches between decks and was described as 'roomy'. Berths were crowded together and until late in the century there were no portholes, the only source of fresh air being a few overhead hatches. Here men, women and children ate, slept, performed the functions of nature, were born and often died. The stench was indescribable, and smallpox and cholera frequently broke out. On some voyages, half the passengers died and the mortality among children was very high.

Those who reached America were free to take up a wide variety of work. Although the unskilled and those whose hopes were dashed in the New World are under-represented in the emigrant letters that survive, the positive reaction of the emigrants to America is impressive. It is interesting to note, however, that although emigrants were often unrestrained in their praise of America, they were cautious about advising others to cross the Atlantic. Relatives arriving from Ulster would naturally have expected suitable hospitality and financial assistance until they had firmly established themselves. The following letter from a Co. Down emigrant in 1785 is typical: 'I have not been at a loss for work nor lost no time since I came to America. As for encouraging any person to come here, I will not, but if any friends or acquaintances comes, I would be glad to see them.'

The attractions of America were avidly recounted in letters home to friends and relatives. On 12 May 1785, John Dunlap, a committed patriot who was responsible for the printing of the Declaration of Independence, wrote to his brother-in-law in Strabane, Co. Tyrone, extolling the advantages of the New World:

> *People with a family advanced in life find great difficulties in emigration, but the young men of Ireland who wish to be free and happy should leave it and come hear as quick as possible. There is no place in the world where a man meets so rich a reward for good conduct and industry as in America.*

By the time of his death in 1812, Dunlop had acquired 98,000 acres in Kentucky and Virginia.

Another drain on the population in the eighteenth century resulted from the enlisting of men for service in the Catholic armies of France and Spain. Known as the Wild Geese, they consisted of family groupings who created closely knit military communities on the Continent and maintained links with Irish merchant and religious bodies there. After the Treaty of Limerick in 1691 approximately 14,000 Jacobite soldiers went to France, where they formed the Irish brigade. Reports of recruiting for the armies of France and Spain were persistent in the early decades of the eighteenth century, and the numbers enlisting were said to be high. In 1721, for example, the government was informed that 2,000 men were waiting in the mountains near Dungarvan for transport to Spain, and that from Cork at least 20,000 had been or were about to be sent to the Continent. In 1729–30 the government considered granting a licence to the French to recruit in Ireland. An officer in the French service, Lieutenant-Colonel Richard Hennessy, came to Dublin with some companions, bearing an introduction from the Duke of Newcastle to Boulter, but news of the scheme leaked out, strong opposition was expressed in England and Ireland and the officers were withdrawn. Thereafter enlisting continued, as before, surreptitiously.

Nineteenth-century emigrants, especially after 1845, were for the most part Catholic. They came mostly from the poorest part of the country, the west, and their emigration was caused by the harsh economic conditions. These emigrants settled, to a large extent, in the eastern cities of America and the number who took up farming was small in proportion to German and Scandinavian emigrants. *The Irish News* (New York) advised Irishmen to go west, where the poorest emigrant could acquire

Emigrants' Departure. Illustrated London News *(1850).*

40 or 80 acres, pay for it in labour and become independent. However, it advised Irishmen not to go to Canada, 'the American Siberia', where everything was inferior to the United States and the country filled with Orangemen.

In the first half of the nineteenth century it was common practice for a young husband (or occasionally a wife) to emigrate alone in the hope of earning or borrowing enough to bring out their family after a year or so. A husband wrote to his Galway wife in 1848:

> *I send home this 10 pound; I hope that it will not be long until I send for ye all. I would make arrangement to send for some of ye, but I expect to bring ye all from Liverpool. I would rather ye would be all together than to separate ye from each other ... I hope that my fine children is all together ... We are all very clean here; every one in this country wash their faces and comes [sic] their hair three times a day.*

It was reported in Longford in 1835 that sometimes 'a married man, driven to despair by his hopeless condition, takes the extreme step of deserting his family, and absconding to America, leaving his wife and children with very slender means of subsistence'; though always with the 'fixed intention' of sending for them when able. During the famine husbands were particularly inclined to exploit the public relief system; able-bodied men would desert their families and 'proceed to America immediately, and probably they are not heard of for months, and a great many when they get out there marry again; they forget that they have wives and families at home, and their wives and families remain as permanent paupers in the workhouse'.

The vast majority of those who fled the famine had to raise the money for their passage. America remained the most popular destination during the famine years. If this could not be raised through the sale of their stock or their interest in the farm there was also the possibility of help from those who had already settled in the United States. Michael Rush of Ardglass, Co. Down, wrote to his parents in America requesting their help:

> *Now my dear father and mother, if you knew what hunger we and our fellow-countrymen are suffering, you could take us out of this*

poverty Isle . . . If you don't endeavour to take us out of it, it will be
the first news you will hear by some friend of me and my little
family to be lost by the hunger, and there are thousands dread they
will share the same fate.

As a means of reducing the numbers of destitute persons, and lessening
the burden of the crippling poor rate on the landowners, the government
gave its wholehearted support to assisted emigration schemes. The Poor
Relief Acts of 1838, 1843, 1847 and 1849 empowered the Boards of
Guardians to raise such sums 'not exceeding the proceeds of one shilling
in the pound' of the annual poor rate to 'assist poor persons who would
otherwise have to be accommodated in the workhouse' to emigrate,
preferably to the British colonies. The Colonial Land and Emigration
Commission was set up in England in 1840, under the control of the
British Colonial Office, to organize and supervise emigration from both
Britain and Ireland. The availability of emigration was constantly brought
to the attention of the Boards of Guardians in circular letters issued
by the Poor Law Commissioners. The representative of the Emigration
Commission visited every workhouse in Ireland to inspect and select
persons for emigration and those chosen were offered a free passage and
supplied before departure with clothing and a little money to support
themselves on arrival.

The guardians also agreed that assisted emigration should be organized
for inmates who had no means of providing support for themselves, such
as single mothers with young children, or female orphans whose parents
had abandoned them in the workhouse. This was largely an extension of
a policy which was already in operation as workhouses in Ulster had
been for a number of years been arranging for inmates, both adult
and children, to emigrate. A letter from Edward Senior, Assistant Poor
Law Inspector, received by Ballymoney and other Ulster workhouses in
April 1849, encourages guardians 'to send as emigrants to Canada any of
the able-bodied inmates, especially females . . . in this move some of the
permanent dead weight in the workhouse may be get rid of at a cost . . . of
about £5 or one year's cost of maintenance'.

By the time of the Great Famine the United States government
had imposed strict controls on its passenger vessels and this had helped
push up fares. Lower standards meant British fares to Canada, as low as

Quarter-Deck. Illustrated London News *(1850)*.

£3 per person, were one-third of the price of going to New York. Vessels carrying goods from St Lawrence and Newfoundland to British ports gladly accepted destitute Irish into their holds as ballast. These were the infamous 'coffin ships', grossly overcrowded and inadequately provided with food and clean water. As a result the famine fever flourished. At Grosse Isle, where a quarantine station had been established, Stephen de Vere noted in his diary 'water covered with beds cooking vessels etc. of the dead. Ghastly appearance of boats full of sick going ashore never to return. Several died between ship and shore. Wives separated from husbands, children from parents, etc'.

After about 1850, as rural society stabilized and the removal of entire households became less common, another model of chain emigration became predominant. In 1852 an Armagh linen merchant, who had handled numerous remittances and 'thousands of their letters', discerned 'almost an organised system' in his locality: 'a son or daughter goes first, acquires some money, and sends it home; ... the money which is sent takes out another member of the family, and at length the whole family go'. This system enabled the surplus children of rural households to emigrate successively.

From the 1850s it was the wealth abroad rather than destitution at home which attracted emigration. As Jules de Lasteryrie wrote in 1860 'it is no longer the destitution of Ireland, but the wealth of Canada, of the United States, and of Australia, which now promotes Irish emigration'. It has been estimated that women formed about half the numbers of those who emigrated during the nineteenth century. Before the Great Famine most travelled as part of a family group or childless married couples. By the late Victorian area females formed a majority of those emigrating. More than half of these were unmarried, leaving by choice, hoping for better prospects in America or the colonies. Most ended up in domestic service – in America it was estimated that as many as 43 per cent of domestic servants were Irish. Figures also suggest that the vast majority of women who emigrated married.

In order to meet the great demand for farmers and agricultural labourers the Canadian government offered assisted passages to married agricultural labourers when accompanied by their families and to servant girls at £2 per adult, £1 for children under one year and 6s 8d for infants under 12 months. In addition the government of Ontario offered free passes from Quebec to any part of the province of Ontario, and a grant to each person 12 years of age and over of the sum of $6 or £1 4s 8d, after three months in the province, and to provide employment with farmers and others for any person requiring it.

Letters written by family already in Canada also played their part in attracting emigrants. One such emigrant was Isaac Topley who wrote to his family at Markethill in Co. Armagh. In a letter postmarked February 1850, with Ireland ravaged by the Great Famine, he declared 'the winter here is very pleasant. I can work with my coat of all day, the winter is getting something like home, the snow is not more than 2 or 3 inches deep this winter as yet, everyday is like a Christmas here for eating and drinking there is so many thing(s) on the table we do not know what to eat ...'

Isaac's brother Abraham, writing to their brother-in-law James Boardman at Tandragee a few years later, passed on news of their sister Elizabeth. He also told them that he was thinking of getting married:

I was thinking of looking for a woman as the people is advising me to marry. I believe I could get one ... she [has] fifty acres of good land and has the deed in her own name but she has four children.

Geordie Ryan's family, Canada.

*She is from Comber below Belfast the people advise me not to take
her on the account of her having a family, so I think I will not heed
it now nor never with the same ...*

In 1871 the first census of the dominion of Canada was taken. The Irish
were found to be 24.3 per cent of the entire population, making them
the argest English-language ethnic group. In Ontario, the heartland of
English-speaking Canada, persons of Irish origins were 34.5 per cent of the
population, by far the largest ethnic group.

Australia emigration, as a mass organized movement did not get going
in a major way until the 1820s, after the disruption of the Napoleonic
Wars. The distance involved, and the logistics of the journey, meant that
the numbers going to Australia as compared with North America were
much smaller. Before the 1830s those who travelled to Australia were
generally better off than those who left Ireland for North America. Few
Irish emigrants could afford the full fare of about £17. Australia, therefore, attracted a significant proportion of emigrants with the resources to
set themselves up in business or on the land in the expanding agricultural
hinterland of the coastal settlements. One such person was Henry
Osborne, who left his father's substantial Co. Tyrone farm in 1828 and
invested the £1,000 his father gave him as a farewell gift in Irish linen
which, on his arrival in Sydney, he is reputed to have sold at a fine profit.
Osborne received two land grants, each of 2,560 acres, at Marshall
Mount. By 1854 Osborne held 261,000 acres, a large portion of which
he leased from the government at less than one-fifth of a penny per year,
including land which contained the valuable coalfields at Newcastle.

By the 1830s there were a number of sponsored or assisted passages.
The following advertisement appeared in the *Londonderry Sentinel* from
July to September 1836:

*Her Majesty's government in order to encourage the emigration
of industrious young married couples to the Australian colonies will
now grant towards the expenses of their passage a bounty or free
gift of £20 for each married couple without regard to their trade
or occupation ... thus a man and wife who are possessed of £18
may be conveyed free to Van Diemen's Land or Sydney with all
provisions for the voyage ...*

After 1856 each of the four main colonies, New South Wales, Tasmania, Victoria and South Australia, developed its own assisted scheme and some had more than one. These ranged from land guarantees to free passages. Recent studies have suggested than 64 per cent of all immigrants up to 1850, 34 per cent in the Gold Rush era and 51 per cent from 1860–1900 were assisted. The Irish were quick to understand the mechanism of assisted migration. Although they formed only about 30 per cent of the total population of the British Isles, they made up 52 per cent of the assisted migrants to New South Wales and to the Port Phillip District (later Victoria) in the period 1837–50.

An earlier source of free passages at central expense was convict transportation. Convicts had been transported, as an alternative to hanging, since the early seventeenth century. Early destinations had been North America and the West Indies. The American War of Independence had brought to an end the transportation to North America and with the jails becoming overcrowded Parliament sanctioned transportation to Australia.

The Queen, the first Irish convict ship, sailed from Cork in April 1791. The number of transportations gathered pace after the economic downturn which followed the end of the Napoleonic Wars. The assize court books for Co. Antrim show a large number of larceny offences for which transportation was adjudged appropriate punishment. For example, for the 130 convictions at the Co. Antrim assizes in Carrickfergus in 1827, 80 were for grand larceny – i.e. theft of goods to the value of more than 12 pence. Of these 40 were sentenced to transportation.

Men, women and children were transported, sometimes for the most trivial offences. A Co. Antrim man, William McKeown, received a seven-year sentence for stealing two and a half yards of cloth. Boys of 12 and under were sent to the penal colonies for pilfering, and women, often with infants or small children, for 'being vagabonds'. Shortly before and immediately after the 1798 Rebellion, a number of United Irishmen were sent out. On the whole the colonial government did not want to be swamped by those who had been involved in seditious activities, fearing that with the transportation of Whiteboys and other agrarian agitators, they would foment revolution in the southern continent. Therefore, according to one Ulster magistrate: 'All United Irishmen who were in on treasonable practices are only indicted for a lesser offence so as to come under transportation . . .'

It has been estimated that, from 1788 to 1853, about 40,000 Irish criminals were shipped directly from Ireland to Australia. Another 8,000 Irish men and women were sent into penal exile from courts in Scotland and England. Convict settlements were a feature of Australian society for nearly a century until the transportation system was progressively withdrawn from 1840 onwards. In that year New South Wales was removed from the system. It was followed by Tasmania in 1852 and Western Australia in 1867. The main reason for this was that the Australian colonists came to regard the convict system as a stigma on those who had chosen to emigrate and there was criticism in both Britain and Australia because of the inevitable brutality of certain aspects of the convict system.

Nevertheless there were many who having travelled to Australia as convicts went on to carve a new and prosperous life for themselves. One such emancipated convict, Robert Boyde, writing from Modbury County, Murray, New South Wales, told his family that: 'I am happy to inform you that I am master of sixteen head of cattle which I have bought at different times with money earned after doing my government work.'

Even those who paid their way could be subjected to something approaching naval discipline during the long voyage. James Dempsey, sailing from Derry in 1838, discovered that 'if anyone is found pilfering . . . or giving insolence . . . or refusing to clean their births or sweep upper and lower decks . . . when they arrived at Sidney, will be given up to the government and punished in proportion'. For those of a more refined nature the amusements on board ship were almost as bad as the brutal discipline. Elizabeth Anketell, from Aughnacloy in Co. Tyrone, was far from amused at the initiation ceremony aimed at those who were 'crossing the line' for the first time. A passenger on the *Queen of Australia*, she complained:

> *I cannot enjoy these nasty jokes – the victim is placed on a stool, held by two men blackened all over to represent Negroes; Neptune and his wife dressed up in the most hideous manner, sit in front. A large brush, dipped in pitch and tar is put all over the face and into the mouth if possible . . . he is rolled down into a tank of sea water and nearly smothered by the two Negroes . . . I had to pay a fine of three shillings and kiss Mrs Neptune – this I certainly did not calculate on.*

It offended her very Victorian sense of propriety when she had put some clothing out to dry that members of the crew hoisted them 'to the highest mast on the ship'. William Bates, a young Presbyterian clergyman from Strabane in Co. Tyrone was equally upset by what he saw as the sudden desertion of spiritual virtues on board ship. He complained that: 'Our young men seem indifferent to religion ... they crowned the Sabbath evening's impropriety by closing Mr Bowman [a fellow cleric] in the water closet, tying the doors together with a rope.'

With the mass exodus of the Great Famine, emigration was to become an important element in Irish society during the next one hundred years. Many travellers to Ireland comment on it. Dr David Forbes, who travelled around Ireland during the autumn of 1852, arrived at Killaloe, twelve miles from Limerick, to join the steamer for a pleasure cruise to Athlone where he came across a party of emigrants. They were all making their way to Liverpool via Dublin. The majority of them were going to the United States, but several, particularly the young women, were bound for Australia. Dr Forbes was moved by the distressing scenes he witnessed at the quayside:

> *With the utter unconsciousness and disregard of being observed of all observers, which characterises authentic sorrow, these warm-hearted and simple-minded people demeaned themselves entirely as if they had been shrouded in all the privacy of home, clinging to and kissing and embracing each other with the utmost ardour, calling out aloud, in broken tones, the endeared names of brother, sister, mother, sobbing and crying as if the very heart would burst, while the unheeded tears ran down form the red and swollen eyes literally in streams.*

More than eight million left Ireland between 1801 and 1921, making it one of the greatest mass migrations in world history: approximately one million people left the country between 1846 and 1850 alone. Those who remained and who survived the Great Famine had to deal with massive social changes brought about by the blight. The ramshackle economy, which had grown up during the Napoleonic Wars, had been destroyed and the persistent problem of unemployment had been eradicated. Uniquely in Europe, Ireland's population shrank from eight million to four million in 1921. Those who left Ireland, whether serving as an administrator in Canada or panning for gold in Australia, ensured the impact of Irish emigration was out of proportion to its status as a small country on the outskirts of Europe. Its chief legacy is that today no less than seventy million people around the world can claim Irish descent.

RESEARCH
GUIDE

A

WHERE TO START

Once bitten by the need to trace your family tree it is very tempting to rush to the nearest archival institution – only to be put off immediately by the daunting amount of information available. It is therefore best to begin your research at home. Start with yourself, work through your parents to your grandparents and take each generation as you find it. Searching through old records, although often rewarding, is apt to be perplexing and frustrating. Even the most experienced researcher can take a wrong turn and end up spending valuable time ploughing through records that only lead to a dead-end. To make more productive use of your time, it is essential to gather as much information as possible from old family Bibles, legal documents (such as wills or leases) and inscriptions from family gravestones. This can help to pinpoint exactly where your family lived at a particular time and provide vital clues to add to names that family historians are often disappointed to find are all too popular in Ireland.

A walk around a graveyard can often save wading through endless pages of a church register for the birth or death dates of a particular ancestor. In Ireland the practice of erecting a headstone to mark the last resting-place of a relative dates in most areas from the seventeenth century. Those that were erected before the seventeenth century tended to be made of wood and so have not survived. If a parish register records the burial of your ancestor in the churchyard, any headstone, if it survives, should be in that churchyard. A death certificate does not indicate the place or date of burial, but your relatives may hold memorial or funeral cards. Because so many headstones can be illegible it is worth checking at your local library to find out if the gravestones in a particular cemetery have been transcribed and published.

Having done your homework you are now ready to tackle the extensive records held in various archival institutions across Ireland. Unlike the British Isles, which has very extensive civil and census records, Irish ancestral research is hampered by the destruction of so many of the major record collections. The family historian in Ireland is forced to make greater use of church records, school registers and land and valuation records than their counterparts in England, Scotland or Wales. Nevertheless, with diligence, the family historian in Ireland should be able to trace their roots to the beginning of the nineteenth century and a lucky few may be able to trace a line further than the early seventeenth century.

To make best use of the records it is essential to know where your ancestors lived in Ireland. Linking your ancestor to a county is a great help, but what you really need to do is to identify the parish or townland of origin. The county-based heritage centres in Ireland can help. Established as part of the Irish Genealogical Project, which aims to create a comprehensive genealogical database for the entire island of Ireland, each centre indexes and computerizes records of a particular county, or in some cases two counties. Staff will search their databases for a fee. If you only know the name of the county your ancestor came from, one of these centres may be the best way of finding a more specific place of origin.

B

CENSUS RECORDS

At first glance, Irish census returns would seem to be an obvious place for family historians to begin their search. The census is basically a head count of every person living in Ireland from the youngest children to the oldest inhabitant of the household. The first properly organized census in Ireland commenced in 1821 and, thereafter, with some exceptions, a census was taken every ten years. Unfortunately, most census returns from 1821 to 1851 were lost during the destruction of the Public Record Office, Dublin, in 1922, and those from 1861 to 1891 were pulped into waste paper during the First World War.

1821 CENSUS

This census was organized by townland, civil parish, barony and county and took place on 28 May 1821. Almost all the original returns were destroyed in 1922, with only a few volumes surviving for Cos. Fermanagh (PRONI MIC/5A and MIC/15A), Cavan, Galway, Meath and King's County (Offaly). You can find call numbers for all of these in the Pre-1901 Census Material catalogue in the NAI. They are also on microfilm (MFGI-34).

1831–4 CENSUS

Again this census was organized by townland, civil parish, barony and county. It also includes the name, age, occupation and religion of the occupants. No original returns survive, but in 1834 the Commissioners of Public Instruction, Ireland, made copies of the original returns, and information survives for Co. Londonderry at PRONI MIC 5A.

The census returns for Londonderry are also available at the NAI. You can find the call numbers in the Pre-1901 Census Material catalogue. An index, compiled by the Derry Inner City Trust, is also available at the NAI on microfiche.

The Commissioners of Public Instruction also instructed clergy of all denominations to conduct censuses in their areas in 1834. Few of these returns are available. The 1834 census of Granard parish in Co. Longford, listing heads of household, is held by the NLI (Pos. 4237). Returns for seven civil parishes in Co. Kerry have been published in the *Journal of the Kerry Archaeological and Historical Society* (1974–5), and those for Templebredin in Cos. Limerick and Tipperary in the *North Muster Antiquarian Journal*, 17 (1975). The censuses for Tallanstown, Co. Louth, published in the *Journal of the Co. Louth Archaeological Society*, 14 (1957), and Kilcumreragh in Cos. Offaly and Westmeath, on microfilm at the NLI (Pos. 1994), appear to be part of this survey.

1841 CENSUS
Some abstracts exist for Co. Monaghan: Thrift Abstracts, NAI. For Cavan, returns survive for part of the parish of Killeshandra and for some households in Cos. Cork, Fermanagh and Waterford are held in the NAI. You can find the call numbers in the Pre-1901 Census Material catalogue.

1851 CENSUS
Most of the surviving returns relate to Co. Antrim and the townland of Clonee in Co. Fermanagh, held at PRONI (MIC 5A/11–26) and the NAI (call numbers are available in the Pre-1901 Census Material catalogue).

There are also individual census returns for various parts of Northern Ireland in PRONI MIC/15A. Some extracts survive for Co. Monaghan: Thrift Abstracts, NAI. Extracts for Aglish, Portnascully and Rathkieran in Co. Kilkenny are at the Genealogical Office (Ms 684). The NAI also has lists of heads of households for Cromac Ward, Belfast (Cen 1851/19) and the city of Dublin (Cen 1851/18/1–2).

Abstracts from the 1841 and 1851 censuses are also available on a CD-ROM, *Irish Source Records*, published by the Genealogical Publishing Company (www.genealogical.com/products/Irish%20Source%20Records/7275.html). The *1851 Dublin City Census, Chart's Index of Heads of Household* CD-ROM compiled and edited by Sen Magee (Eneclann, 2001) is also recommended.

1861, 1871, 1881 AND 1891 CENSUSES
The census records for 1861 to 1891 were destroyed by order of the government during the First World War.

1901 CENSUS
On 31 March 1901, a census was taken of the whole island of Ireland. The original returns are deposited at the NAI; microfilm copies of the returns for Northern Ireland are available at PRONI. Every town, village and townland in Ireland is represented and those inhabitants who were at home on 31 March 1901 are listed.

A catalogue of the original census returns is held at the NAI on the open shelves in the Reading Room. Each county is listed in a separate volume. The records are numerically arranged by district electoral division (DED) and held in bound volumes. Before consulting the 1901 census returns, you must establish in which DED the relevant townland or street is situated. The DED was a subdivision of the old poor law union and was used for electoral purposes. The DED, with a number attached, can be found in the 1901 *Townland Index*, which is available on the shelves of the Search Room. Simply look up the relevant townland, village or town and you will find it listed along with the barony and poor law union.

Within each DED the townlands are arranged alphabetically and numerically. In order to request the returns for a particular townland you must include the name of the county, the number of the DED and the number of the townland.

The 1901 census is available on microfilm at PRONI under reference MIC/354. Once again it is necessary to find out the relevant DED. This can be done by consulting the 1901 *Townland Index*, which is available on the shelves of the Search Room. Each DED is listed in a series of calendars which will give you the appropriate reel number.

1911 CENSUS

The 1911 census was taken on 1 April of that year and includes, in addition to the information in the 1901 census, the number of years a wife had been married, the number of children born and the number still living. This census is not yet available at PRONI because of the more restrictive UK 'hundred year closure rule' on access, but microfilms of the original census returns can be viewed at the NAI.

In order to locate the relevant DED number, the townland, town or street number it is necessary to consult the 1911 census catalogue, available on the open shelves in the NAI. Sometimes this number corresponds with the number used in 1901, but in many cases it does not. If the 1911 DED number cannot be found, help should be sought from the Search Room staff.

It is important to realize that there were boundary changes in townlands and DEDs between 1901 and 1911; an official Parliamentary Paper listing these changes was published. Unlike the 1901 census returns, which are held in large bound volumes, those for 1911 are unbound and stored in folders within boxes.

1901 AND 1911 CENSUSES ONLINE

On 6 December 2005, John O'Donoghue, Irish Minister for Arts, Sports and Tourism, announced the signing of an agreement between the NAI and the Library and Archives Canada, which will have great significance for all researchers with Irish roots. Under this agreement the Irish census records for 1901 and 1911 will be digitized, indexed over a three-year period and placed online for free access, making it considerably easier for the more than 70 million people of Irish descent around the world to retrace their families and heritage.

The Irish Census Project will digitize over 3,000 census microfilm reels, and create two indexes linked to the digital images: a topographical index based on townland/street within DEDs, and a nominal index to every individual listed in both censuses. Those for Dublin are now available at www.census.nationalarchives.ie and the rest will be added over time.

C

BIRTH, DEATH AND MARRIAGE RECORDS

BIRTH CERTIFICATES

The first significant evidence of the life of an individual born since 1864 is his or her birth certificate. From this we can learn where a person was born, the names of the parents, the maiden name of the mother and the occupation of the father. This gives the researcher many important clues with which to move back to a previous generation.

Birth certificates normally give the name of the child, but in some cases only the sex is recorded, i.e. the child had not been given a name by the time the birth was registered. The name and residence of the father are registered. Although the latter is usually the same as the place of birth of the child, in some cases it will show that the father was working abroad or in another part of Ireland when the child was born. The mother's maiden name is provided as well as her first name. Finally, the name and address of the informant are recorded, together with his or her qualification to sign. This person will usually be the father or mother or someone present at the birth, such as a midwife or even the child's grandmother.

It is important to treat the dates on Irish birth certificates with a degree of caution. As a general rule, the younger the child was when registered, the more accurate the birthdate written in the official register. The longer families waited to register the child the more chance that the date given is inaccurate. Families were also prepared to change the date of birth if the child was more than three months old to avoid paying the late registration penalty.

MARRIAGE CERTIFICATES
Civil records of marriage normally give fuller information than birth and death certificates, and are the most useful of the civil records. Information on the individuals getting married includes their name, age, status and occupation. The names and occupations of their fathers are also given. The church, the officiating minister and the witnesses to the ceremony are named. In most cases the exact age of the parties is not registered, and the entry will simply read 'full age' (i.e. over 21) or 'minor' (i.e. under 21). If the father of one of the parties was no longer living this may be indicated in the marriage certificate, but in many cases it is not. The fact that marriage certificates had to be filed within three days of the marriage ceremony means that marriage dates are generally accurate.

DEATH CERTIFICATES
Civil records of death in Ireland are sadly rather uninformative. The name of the deceased is given together with the date, place and cause of death, marital status, the age of death, and occupation. The name and address of the informant is also recorded. Usually this is the person present at the time of the death, who may be a close family member or even an employee or servant.

THE INDEXES
Indexes to civil marriages 1845–63 are handwritten, but thereafter all indexes are printed. From 1864 to 1877 indexes for births, marriages and deaths consist of a single yearly volume covering the whole of Ireland. Records for the years 1878 to 1903 are divided into four quarters ending March, June, September and December. It is therefore necessary to check the index for each quarter in any one year. Births which were registered late are at the back of the index for each year. From 1903 to 1927, in 1933, and from 1966 to 1995 births reverted to being indexed annually.

In all years indexed annually, late registrations are given after 'Z'. The name of the superintendent registrar's district is also given, followed by the volume number and page number of the master copies of the registers in Dublin.

GENERAL REGISTER OFFICE, DUBLIN

The General Register Office (Oifig An Ard-Chlaraitheora) is the civil repository for records relating to births, death and marriages in the Republic of Ireland.

Indexes are currently in a manual format so accurate dates are required. Three types of index contain entries relating to birth, death or marriage records and cover the following periods:

- Birth indexes – 1864 onwards
- Death indexes – 1864 onwards
- Marriage indexes –1845 onwards

Only the indexes are available for public inspection, not the records themselves. The Public Office and Research Room are open from Monday to Friday (excluding public holidays) from 9.30 am to 4.30 pm for the purpose of searching the indexes to birth, death and marriage records and obtaining certificates. A particular search covering a maximum of five years costs €1.90: a general search for one day covering all years costs €15.24.

The General Register Office is located at Joyce Hose, 8–11 Lombard Street, Dublin 2. Applications for certificates can be made in person, by post, by telephone or online (www.grioreland.ie/applu_for_a_cert.htm).

GENERAL REGISTER OFFICE, BELFAST, AND DISTRICT REGISTRAR'S OFFICES

The General Register Office (GRO) in Belfast holds the original birth and death registers recorded by the local district registrars for Northern Ireland from 1864. Marriage registers are available from 1922. The following computerized indexes to the civil registers are available:

- Birth indexes – 1864 onwards
- Death indexes – 1864 onwards
- Marriage indexes – 1845 onwards

A general search of records assisted by members of GRO staff for any period of years and any number of entries costs £24 per hour.

If you wish to search the indexes yourself (only indexes are available for public inspection, not the registers themselves) it is possible to visit the GRO if you have arranged a time and date in advance. An index search costs £10 for a period not exceeding six hours. This includes four verifications of items found in the indexes, with the option of further verifications at £2.50 each. A full certified copy of a birth, death or marriage certificate costs £11.

The General Register Office is located at Oxford House, 49–55 Chichester Street, Belfast BT1 4HL. Applications for certificates can be made in person, by post, by telephone (028 9025 2000) or online (www.groni.gov.uk). Searches will be made in the year quoted plus the two years either side unless a wider search is requested. A further fee will be required for each extra five years searched. Personal applications are processed within three working days; postal or telephone applications are processed within eight working days.

Although indexes to civil marriages registers for Northern Ireland are available at the GRO from 1845, the original registers are located at the district registrar's offices at local councils. Applications for marriage certificates can be made directly to them or through the GRO in Belfast.

CHURCH OF LATTER-DAY SAINTS

From 1948 the Church of the Latter-Day Saints (LDS), or Mormons, began microfilming documentary material in Ireland. The most important resources acquired at that time were the registers of births, deaths and marriages as well as the indexes to these records held in the Registrar General's Office, Custom House, Dublin. Unfortunately the Mormons were not able to complete the filming of all registers before work was suspended.

The LDS collection of microfilms of civil registers and indexes contains:

- Birth indexes – 1864–1959
- Birth registers – 1864 to first quarter 1880; 1900–1913
- Marriage indexes – 1845–1959
- Marriage registers – 1845–70

- Death indexes – 1864–1959
- Death registers – 1864–70

It is important to note that, although there are gaps in the birth registers, microfilm copies of the actual official registers are available to researchers. This is a vital resource, because in the General Register Offices in Dublin, Belfast and London the public have no right of access to the original records. In addition, some parts of the early years of birth registrations appear in the LDS *International Genealogical Index*, which is searchable online (www.familysearch.org/), and the 2002 edition of the LDS CD set *British Isles Vital Records* includes an index to birth registrations from 1864 to 1875.

Access to microfilmed copies of the indexes and registers is also free of charge at any of the LDS Family History Centres. The Family History Library catalogue is the best way to find collections in the Family History Library. It is usual to search by place to find the records available for where your ancestors lived. The records are listed by country, county or civil parish, depending on the nature of the records. Within each locality, the records are organized by topic – in this case 'Civil registration'.

D

CENSUS SUBSTITUTES

SEVENTEENTH-CENTURY MUSTER ROLLS

A muster roll was a list of able-bodied men who were capable of military service. These men were armed at their own expense. The muster rolls for 1642–3 were compiled following the outbreak of the 1641 rebellion and represent the settler response to the crisis. Muster rolls contain lists of the principal landlords in Ulster, and the names of the men they could assemble in an emergency. The Armagh County Museum copy is available in the NLI (Positive microfilm 206). PRONI also holds copies on microfilm (MIC/15A/52–53 and 73).

A muster roll for Ulster for 1630 is held by the British Museum (Add. Ms 4770). Copies are held by PRONI (MIC/339) and NLI (n.12p.296), and by major libraries such as the Linen Hall Library and Central Library, Belfast.

DEPOSITIONS, 1641

The depositions of 1641 are the collected accounts of witnesses to the robberies and murders that took place during the rebellion of that year. Eight Protestant clergymen, led by Henry Jones, Dean of Kilmore, were empowered to take evidence during two commissions in December 1641 and January 1642. In 1652, following Cromwell's subjugation of the country, a High Court of Justice was established to collect evidence for the trials of those who had risen against the settlers.

Most of the witnesses were English settlers and their occupations ranged from 'gentleman' to 'tanner', 'tailor' and 'inn keeper'. They named their attackers, or those rumoured to have taken part in the rising, and the depositions provide rare documentary evidence of the native Irish families who had once dominated the country. The original depositions for Cos. Antrim, Armagh, Cavan, Down, Monaghan and Tyrone are deposited in the library of Trinity College, Dublin (Ms 837). Copies of the 1641 depositions are available at PRONI (D/1923, T/2706/8 and MIC/8/1). Copies are also held in the NAI (n.4579p.4545). Trinity College recently announced a one-million-euro three-year digital imaging project which will make the depositions available online.

POLL TAX, 1660s
The Poll Tax was levied at irregular intervals mainly to provide money for military purposes. An Ordinance of the General Convention dated 24 April 1660 stated 'every person above the age of fifteen years of either sex ... under the degree or quality of yeoman, or farmer yeoman, or farmer's wife or widow shall pay twelve pence'. The sums payable by gentlemen, esquires, knights, barons, earls and others were then specified in an ascending scale. The Poll Tax returns give detailed facts about individuals quite unique in surviving seventeenth-century records. Copies of the surviving records are held by the major archives in Dublin and Belfast.

CENSUS OF IRELAND, c.1659
Sir William Petty's surveyors probably made the census of 1659. Petty, described by Samuel Pepys as 'the most intelligent man I know', arrived in Ireland in 1652 as physician-general to Cromwell's armies. He soon abandoned medicine in order to concentrate on cartography, surveying and economics and was made responsible for mapping all the 2,800,000 acres of land confiscated after the Cromwellian victory in Ireland. It was the first systematic survey of Ireland, requiring 1,000 assistants, and in many ways was a forerunner of the Ordnance Survey.

The census of 1659 contains only the names of those with title to land (tituladoes) and the total number of English and Irish residents in each townland (Scots were usually counted with English). Five counties, Cavan, Galway, Mayo, Tyrone and Wicklow, are not covered. An edition of the census by Seamus Pender was published in 1939 by the Stationery Office, Dublin, on behalf of the Irish Manuscripts Commission. This includes a breakdown of the figures for each county and an index of both personal names and place names. Copies of Petty's census are held by the National Library (NLI 6551), and on microfilm by PRONI (MIC/15/A and T/808).

SUBSIDY ROLLS, 1663–1666

Subsidy rolls list the nobility, clergy and laity who paid grants in aid to the Crown. The surviving lists, relating largely to Ulster, are made up of those of means in the community who were subject to the payment of subsidies, which then formed the government's main method of direct taxation. They include the amount paid and the status of the person.

An index to the names of persons listed in the 1663 subsidy roll is available on the shelves of the Public Search Room at PRONI and a copy is available (T/307). Copies are also available at the NLI (Ms 9584/5) and NAI (M 2745).

HEARTH MONEY ROLLS

Arranged by county and parish, these list the name of the householder and the number of hearths on which he was taxed, at the rate of 2 shillings on every hearth or fireplace. Its unpopularity led to its abolition in England and Wales after the Glorious Revolution of 1688. In Ireland it continued to be levied until the Act of Union in 1800. The original Hearth Money Rolls were destroyed in the Four Courts in 1922. Fortunately the Presbyterian Historical Society of Ireland had preserved copies of the rolls for the mid-1660s and copies are now held by all major Irish archives.

'CENSUS OF PROTESTANT HOUSEHOLDERS', 1740

What has generally been termed a 'census of Protestant householders' was compiled in 1740. It is no more than a list of names arranged by county, barony and parish and, reflecting its supervision by the inspector responsible for collecting hearth money. The original records of this survey were destroyed in Dublin in 1922 but copies survive for part of the survey in transcripts prepared by the genealogist Tension Groves.

Copies are held by PRONI (T/808/15258) and the NLI (Ms 4173). A bound transcript copy is available on the open shelves of the Public Search Room at PRONI.

THE RELIGIOUS CENSUS, 1766

In March and April 1766, Church of Ireland rectors were instructed by the government to compile complete returns of all householders in their respective parishes, showing their religion, distinguishing between Church of Ireland (Episcopalians), Roman Catholic (termed 'Papists' in the returns) and Presbyterians (or Dissenters), and giving an account of any Roman Catholic clergy active in their area. Some of the more diligent rectors listed every townland and every household, but many drew up only numerical totals of the population. All the original returns were destroyed in the Public Record Office in 1922, but extensive transcripts, again made by Tension Groves, survive for the parishes of Seapatrick, Tullynakill, Greyabbey, Inch and Kilbroney. A bound copy can be found on the shelves of the Public Search Room at PRONI.

Copies of the 1766 Householders List can also be found at the Linen Hall Library, Belfast; Armagh Museum; the Representative Church Body Library, Dublin (Ms 23); NLI (Ms 4173); and at Family History Centres across Ireland (LDS film 1279330). Some originals and transcripts are available at the Genealogical Office (GO 537). A full listing of all surviving manuscripts is available on the shelves of the Reading Room of the NAI.

PETITION OF PROTESTANT DISSENTERS, 1775

The Petition of Protestant Dissenters is a list of names of Dissenters (or Presbyterians) on either a parish or a congregational basis which were submitted to the government in October and November 1775.

Transcript copies are located on the shelves of PRONI (T/808/14977). The NLI reference is Ms 4173.

CATHOLIC QUALIFICATION ROLLS

During the eighteenth century, restrictions enacted by the Penal Laws were relaxed for those Catholics who took the Oath of Allegiance and so 'qualified'. In 1774 an Act was passed to permit the King's subjects of whatever religion to take an oath at the local assize to testify their loyalty and allegiance to him and to promote peace and industry in the kingdom. Records of the more than 1,500 Roman Catholics who took the oath under the 1774 Act, and subsequent Acts of 1782, 1792 and 1793, are found in the Catholic qualification rolls. The original lists were destroyed in 1922, but a transcript was published as an appendix to the *59th Deputy Keeper's Report*. Indexes to the Catholic qualification rolls, 1778–90 and 1793–6, are held in the NAI (n.1898–9p.1898–9).

THE FLAXSEED PREMIUM, 1796
In 1796, as part of a government initiative to encourage the linen industry in Ireland, free spinning-wheels or looms were granted to farmers who planted a certain acreage of their holdings with flax. The names of over 56,000 recipients of these awards have survived in printed form arranged by county and parish. The only copy of the book listing the names of these recipients known to exist until recently was held in the Linen Hall Library, Belfast. Another copy has now been acquired by the Irish Linen Centre in Lisburn Museum. The Ulster Historical Foundation has indexed this source and it is available on a searchable database on the UHF website (www.ancestryireland.com). Recipients from Kerry are also available online at www.rootsweb.com/~irlker/flax1796.html. A micro-fiche index is available in the NAI and PRONI.

THE ULSTER COVENANT, 1912
Prime Minister H H Asquith introduced the third Home Rule Bill to the House of Commons on 11 April 1912. It provided for a parliament in Dublin with limited powers, and it met with strong opposition from Ulster Unionists, who saw it as the first step to Irish independence. On 'Ulster Day', 28 September 1912, the Ulster Covenant was signed by 237,368 men and 234,046 women who pledged themselves to use 'all means which may be found necessary to defeat the present conspiracy to set up a Home Rule Parliament in Ireland'.

The Ulster Covenant signatories of 1912 are an invaluable, if under-used, genealogical resource at PRONI (D/1098). The list includes not simply names but also street addresses, townlands, etc. The signatures have been indexed by PRONI and a searchable database is available on its website (www.PRONI.gov.uk).

E

WILLS AND TESTAMENTARY RECORDS

Once the date of death of an ancestor has been discovered, it is worth finding out whether they left a will. Wills contain not only the name, address and occupation of the testator, but also details of the larger family network, such as cousins and nephews.

One should not assume that because the family was poor members would not have made a will. Sometimes those who made a will were determined that their money or possessions went to the right person when they died. Strangely it doesn't always follow that people who were in comfortable positions left wills. People from well-to-do families sometimes disposed of their wealth before they died in order to avoid death duties.

ADMINISTRATION OF WILLS

Between 1536 and 1858, the Church of Ireland was responsible for all wills and administrations in Ireland. The Probate Act of 1857 transferred probate authority from the Church of Ireland to the newly founded government probate districts. The Church of Ireland subsequently transferred their wills and administration records to the Public Record Office in Dublin. Most wills from before 1900 – some dating from the early sixteenth century – were destroyed when, in 1922, the Public Record Office was bombed during the Irish Civil War. Luckily, will indexes and administration indexes survived and copies of most wills after 1858 were preserved.

WILLS BEFORE 1858

Prior to 1858 the Church of Ireland was responsible for administering all testamentary affairs. Ecclesiastical or consistorial courts in each diocese were responsible for granting probate and conferring on the executors the power to administer the estate. Each court was responsible for wills and administrations in its own diocese. You can use Brian Mitchell's *A New Genealogical Atlas of Ireland*, which has county maps that associate civil parishes with Church of Ireland dioceses, to identify the diocese in which your ancestor lived. Researchers should also bear in mind that when the estate included property worth more than £5 in another diocese, responsibility for the will or administration passed to the prerogative court under the authority of the Archbishop of Armagh.

Indexes to those wills destroyed in 1922 are available on the shelves of the Search Rooms at PRONI and the NAI. These are useful, for although the will cannot now be produced, the index contains the name and residence of the testator and the date that the will was either made or probated. Occasionally the testator's occupation is given.

The NAI holds the Inland Revenue Annual Indexes to Irish Will Registers and Indexes to Irish Administration Registers from 1828 to 1879. The NAI also holds the actual Inland Revenue Irish Will Registers and Irish Administration Registers for the years 1828–39 and Charitable Donations and Bequests will extract books containing abstracts of wills which made charitable bequests, 1800–1961 (there is a separate card index for the period 1800–58 in the Reading Room). Grant books indexes in eight volumes for the years 1811–34 and 1835–58 (accession 999/611) are likewise available.

In addition, many thousands of copies of wills probated before 1858 have been collected over the years by both the NAI and PRONI. The NAI has indexed these in the main Testamentary Card Index in the Reading Room). A card index for pre-1858 surviving wills and will abstracts is also available in the Public Search Room at PRONI. This is arranged alphabetically by the name of the testator and provides the references to wills or extracts from wills that are scattered throughout PRONI collections. Altogether PRONI has over 13,000 copies and abstracts of pre-1858 wills.

There are manuscript indexes to the consistorial and prerogative courts at the NAI. Some indexes have been published. The most important is the *Index to Prerogative Wills, 1536–1810*, edited by Sir Arthur Vicars and published in 1897. This very important reference work for genealogists lists the full name, residence, title or occupation, and date of probate, for almost 40,000 names. It is a particularly important index for the Irish researcher because it serves as a guide to the names that can be found in *Betham's Abstracts*. There are also genealogical pedigree charts available that were derived from Betham's notes, and added to by many other persons, in the Irish Genealogical Office.

You can also consult the Eneclann CD-ROM, *Indexes to Irish Wills, 1484–1858*, which can be purchased online at www.ancestry.com or at www.eneclann.ie. This CD-ROM contains over 70,000 entries from surviving wills, administrations, transcriptions and abstracts.

WILLS 1858–1900

From 1858 district probate courts took over responsibility for wills and administrations from the Church of Ireland. The twelve probate registries created at the time were: the Principal Registry in Dublin and eleven district registries in Armagh, Ballina, Belfast, Cavan, Cork, Kilkenny, Limerick, Londonderry, Mullingar, Tuam and Waterford. The wills of wealthier members of society tended to be probated at the Principal Registry.

The district registries made transcripts of the wills that they proved and of the administrations intestate that they granted before the annual transfer of original records (20 or more years old) to the Public Record Office of Ireland in Dublin. The original wills were destroyed in Dublin in 1922 but the transcripts in will books survived. These are now on deposit in the NAI and PRONI, where they are available on microfilm for the period 1858–1900. Each volume contains an alphabetical index.

WILL CALENDARS

There is no comprehensive index to these post-1858 wills and grants. However, there are bound annual indexes called 'calendars' at both the NAI and PRONI. These calendars are of value to genealogists since they provide the name, address, occupation and date of death of the testator as well as the names, addresses and occupations of executors, the value of estate and the place and date of probate. Even if you have only an approximate date for the death of an ancestor it is worth looking through a number of volumes in the hope of spotting an entry giving details of their will.

When you are using these calendars to gain access to a will or transcript, the vital date to note is neither the date when the will was signed nor the date of death. It is the date of probate, i.e. the date when the will was officially proved in a probate registry. This date of probate is normally a few months after the person died. However, it is well to bear in mind that a significant number of wills were probated ten or more years after death. Such delays may have been more common where probate was in the Principal Registry in Dublin.

A consolidated index to the calendars for 1858–77 is available in the NAI and at PRONI. This gives the year and the registry where the will was probated. These are now online at PRONI and can be searched by surname. Details provided include date of death and abstract of will or letters of administration (see http://www.proni.gov.uk/).

PRONI also has a card index to post-1858 surviving wills and will abstracts. This index is most useful when you are looking for a copy or abstract of a will probate at the Principal Registry in Dublin, as the originals would have been destroyed in 1922 without a transcript being made.

WILLS FROM 1900

The NAI holds original wills and administration papers lodged in the Principal Registry since 1904 and in most district registries, outside Northern Ireland, since 1900. PRONI has in its custody all wills for the districts of Belfast and Londonderry from 1900 to (at present) the mid-1990s, and for Armagh from 1900 until its district registry closed in 1921. Post-1900 original wills and their associated papers are available filed in a separate envelope for each testator. If an individual did not make a will there may be letters of administration that give the name, residence and occupation of the deceased as well as the name and address of the person or persons appointed to administer the estate. Post-1900 wills may be found by using the annual will calendars.

F

SCHOOL RECORDS

U nfortunately, few school records have survived from the eighteenth and early nineteenth centuries. More details of early school records for Northern Ireland can be found in PRONI's *Guide to Educational Records*.

The records produced by the national school system can be divided into two sections: those made centrally by the National Board of Education and those which were made on a local level by the individual schools. The former are split between the NAI and PRONI. When the records were divided, some classes could not be easily split into those relevant to Northern Ireland and those relevant to the twenty-six counties. For this reason, some classes of documents which cover Northern Ireland, such as the teachers' salary books, remain in the NAI.

SCHOOL REGISTERS

Registers generally date from the 1860s and they record information about each pupil: their full name; date of birth (or age on entry); religion; occupation of father and address of parents; details of attendance and academic progress; and the name of the school previously attended. A space is also provided in the registers for general comments, which might tell you where the children went to work afterwards or if they emigrated. Some registers have an index at the front which can greatly ease searching.

In many ways the information contained in the registers for this period can compensate for the lack of census records in the nineteenth century. PRONI has published a *Guide to Educational Records*, which includes an alphabetical list of all the schools for which it holds records. This is available on the shelves of the Public Search Room.

For those tracing ancestors in areas now part of the Republic of Ireland, things are considerably more complex. The vast majority of school registers remain in the custody of local schools or churches. Parish priests also hold some national school registers. Few have lodged their records in the NAI. Those that have include schools in Celbridge, Co. Kildare, Corlespratten, Co. Cavan, and Glenaniff, Co. Leitrim. Some collections of correspondence relating to national schools have also found their way into the NAI. These include Ballyeaston, Co. Antrim, Ardrahan, Co. Galway, and Clonvaraghan, Co. Down. The registers of Denmark Street National School, Dublin, are available in the NAI on microfilm.

The most important accession of national school records the NAI has made recently was from the Representative Church Body. It consists of the records of sixteen national schools, sent there along with various collections of Church of Ireland parochial records. Ten of them have registers which start before the turn of the century. These are Drung and Maghera in Co. Cavan, Robertson's Parochial National School (Civil Parish of Raphoe) in Co. Donegal, St Stephen's (Civil Parish of St Peter) in Dublin City, Tuam Mall in Co. Galway, Cahirciveen in Co. Kerry, Rathmore in Co. Longford, Banagher in Queen's County, Drumbawn in Co. Tipperary and Inch in Co. Wexford.

You can view the lists for roll books and registers, lists for which are arranged by county, at www.nationalarchives.ie/topics/Nat_Schools/natschs.html

SALARY BOOKS

Salary books (NAI, ED4) are of particular interest to researchers with ancestors who worked in the national school system – there are over 1,700 salary books for the period 1834–1918. Teachers are listed under their schools and their salary, rank and other miscellaneous career details are given.

From 1834 to 1844 each volume covers the entire country. From 1844 to 1855 volumes are arranged by county and after that by district. Within these volumes, the arrangement is numerical by school roll. The school roll number may be obtained in the card index in the NAI Reading Room. Unfortunately, there is no personal name index so it is usually necessary to know the school, or at least the area, a teacher taught in before attempting to find records of his/her career.

In addition to giving details of salary, salary books give the exact title of the job, for example, drawing master, medical attendant or principal. Comments about the teacher's career are abundant; details of transfers, retirement or emigration are common.

Salary books for the model schools (ED5) contain the same kind of information as ED4.

G

LANDED ESTATE COLLECTIONS

Estate papers are an invaluable source for family historians. It is not uncommon to find that the records of a single estate have been deposited in more than one archival institution. The family may have donated the papers in their possession to one institution, while those retained by an estate office or solicitor may have been passed on to another. Nevertheless, estate papers offer the best opportunity to trace ancestors into the eighteenth and even seventeenth centuries. They include information not only on the great families who once dominated Irish society, but also on the army of servants, tenants, labourers, shopkeepers and craftsmen with which they came into contact. One of the main items of expenditure on many of the larger estates was servants' wages, for no Irish big house was complete without a large array of retainers, most drawn from the locality, details of which can be found in wage books and household accounts.

The quality of estate papers varies enormously from estate to estate but many include leases, rentals, deeds, maps and correspondence covering every aspect of life on the estate. As a general rule the records of the larger, better managed estates have tended to have a better survival rate than those of smaller concerns.

A landlord granted a lease to a tenant, who was given the right to occupy the property for a specific period of time. Two copies of the lease were usually prepared. The original lease was signed by the landlord and kept by the tenant. The counterpart was signed by the tenant and kept by the landlord. A lease was usually for a term of years: one, twenty-one, fifty or ninety-nine years. The maximum term of a Roman Catholic lease was thirty-one years until the 1778 Act altered this.

Tenants often sublet the property, or part of it, to a third party; this was known as a sublease. The third party became an undertenant, paying rent to the tenant, who continued to pay rent to the landlord. A sub-tenant may not be picked up in the records of the estate, and this can be frustrating when you know that an ancestor leased land in a particular area. It is therefore worthwhile examining the correspondence between a landlord and his agent because this can be of immense genealogical value. Not only does it include details of the day-to-day running of the estate, but mention is often made of those who worked on the estate.

Estate ledgers contain records with particulars of rentals, long- and short-term leases, names of heirs in cases of leases for lives in two or three generations, assignments and fines upon the fall of a life, the death being noted. There are frequently lists of tenants at will or of those who held leases of less than three years' duration. Full rent rolls, dated from time to time, contain the names of the tenants, names of the leased lands (townlands) or parts thereof held by each, the conditions of tenure, including valuation of the property, the length of each lease and provisions for renewal, the annual rent and fines due, and the amount of the paid or unpaid balance. Landlords or estate agents often kept tithe lists, voters' lists, seventeenth-century muster rolls and notes concerning family alliances and the character of various tenants.

Rentals allow local historians to trace individual tenants and over a period of time show how one plot of land or property changed hands. Records were generally arranged by year (rents were usually paid half-yearly) or with several years covered by the same volume. The information provided will usually be limited to the name of the tenant, the extent and location of his holding and the rent payable by him.

FINDING ESTATE RECORDS

For anyone who thinks that their ancestor may have been a tenant farmer on one of the many landed estates in Ireland, it is first of all necessary to identify which estate it may have been. The easiest way to identify the name of a landowner is to examine Griffith's Valuation of *c.*1860 for the relevant townland and note the name of the immediate lessor. For the names of landowners in the early nineteenth century the *Ordnance Survey Memoirs* of the 1830s can be consulted.

The Irish Manuscript Commission carried out a programme aimed at surveying all collections of estate papers in private hands whose owners were willing to have them examined. A report was written on each collection. Representative samples of these reports were published in *Analecta Hibernica*, 15, 20 and 25. The entire collection of reports is available for examination at the Genealogical Office, 2 Kildare Street, Dublin.

Each report consists of a number of foolscap-size typescript pages, bound in volumes. *Analecta Hibernica*, 20, contains a names index keyed to the reports. A list of the reports made up to 1965 is given in *Analecta Hibernica*, 23 and those made since that date are listed in *Analecta Hibernica*, 32 (1985). If there is a report on the estate papers of the landlord you are researching, his name will appear in one of the lists along with the number of the relevant report.

Estate records are held by repositories throughout Ireland including PRONI, the NAI, NLI, Trinity College, Dublin, the Boole Library at NUI, Cork, the Hardiman Library at NUI, Galway, and the Cork Archives Institute. Some are deposited in local libraries and museums. The extent of these collections can be judged in PRONI's *Guide to Estate Collections*, published in 1994. The Personal Names Index in the Public Search Room can also be consulted under the landowner's name. Examples of some of the larger estate collections can found on PRONI's website at www.proni.gov.uk/records/landed.htm

With many of the great landed families owning land on both sides of the Irish Sea, Irish estate records are also held in British archives. Indeed, in the case of absentee or semi-absentee landowners who had estates in Ireland and Britain, estate collections can be scattered amongst a number of repositories. This will require greater detective work on the part of the family historian, who will need to find out where the records have finally been deposited. Most county record offices in Britain publish summary guides to their holdings on the internet and copies of the detailed reports and calendars are available centrally in the National Register of Archives maintained by the UK National Archives at www.nationalarchives.gov.uk/nra

Marriage and inheritance have ensured that many Irish estate papers remain in private hands and outside Ireland. Material relating to the properties of the O'Briens, Earls of Thomond, in Cos. Carlow and Clare, for example, is held in Petworth House, West Sussex. Private owners in both Ireland and Britain vary in their willingness to allow access to their collections.

There are a number of works of reference available, particularly for the second half of the nineteenth century, which will enable the family historian to locate the relevant estate (at least on a county basis). The most important of these are John Bateman, *The Great Landowners of Great Britain and Ireland* (reprinted with an introduction by David Spring, Leicester, 1971) and U H Hussey De Burgh, *The Landowners of Ireland: an Alphabetical List of the Owners of Estates of 500 Acres or £500 Valuation and Upwards in Ireland* (Dublin, 1881).

For the nineteenth century a variety of gazetteers and directories are available which offer some information on landowners in an area. The most useful gazetteer for pre-Famine Ireland is Samuel Lewis, *A Topographical Dictionary for Ireland* (2 vols, London, 1837). It is organized on a county basis and parishes within each county are in alphabetical order. Directories such as *Thom's*, *Slater's* or *Pigot's* also provide some information on estates. *Slater's*, for example, provides lists of the prominent nobility and gentry families in each area. There are also directories which deal with individual counties.

Richard J. Hayes's *Manuscript Sources for the History of Ireland Civilization* is one of the surest ways of locating estate records. For the family historian the most relevant volumes are 1–4, dealing with persons, and 7–8, dealing with place. In these volumes the researcher should look up the name of the landlord or the name of the area(s) where the estate was located. Because landlords tended to have titles and unusual surnames, the problem of confusion over common surnames is not as serious as it is with tenants. Hayes gives the name of the repository in which the estate papers are stored and occasionally a brief list of the documents in the collection. Some repositories will supply a full list, from which one can order selected items.

Collections in provincial and national archives are also summarized in the excellent *Directory of Irish Archives* by Seamus Helferty and Raymond Refausse.

IRISH LAND COMMISSION

The Land Commission was set up in 1881 under the Land Act of that year. Its main function became the advancement of money to tenants to enable them to purchase their holdings and the fixing of fair rents under the various Land Acts from 1881 onwards. Because the Commission had to be satisfied that potential purchasers would be able to repay their annuities, it employed inspectors to assess the capacity of tenants to make their repayments. Therefore, the Land Commission records are one of the few sources which reveal as much about the tenants as about landlords.

Deposited records of the (now defunct) Irish Land Commission held by the NAI date from the seventeenth century onwards, but are not yet catalogued or generally available for public inspection. The records, contained in some 50,000 boxes, were amassed as a result of the operation of the Irish Land Purchase Acts 1881–1923. Records include deeds dating from the seventeenth century, tenants' purchase agreements and resale maps and other records created under the auspices of the numerous administrative branches of the Land Commission.

The best existing search aid was compiled by the NLI, entitled 'Records in the Irish Land Commission: Survey and Guide', and takes the form of typescript volumes and card indexes (accessible only in the NLI). An index to the wills and administrations (which simply gives the name and address and the date of grant of probate or letters of administration) is available on the shelves in the Public Search Room in PRONI. By writing to the Keeper of Records, Land Commission, Bishop Street, Dublin 8, you may be allowed to examine the schedules of areas and accompanying maps but without special permission you cannot access the remaining material.

The records of the Irish Land Commission concerning sales of estates in Northern Ireland to tenants were transferred from Dublin to Belfast in 1922 and were subsequently deposited in the Land Registry archive (LR/1) at PRONI. The Land Registry archive, which contains an estimated 50,000 items, is one of the largest held in PRONI and contains numerous classes of records which will be of interest to genealogists. Title deeds, for example, relate to the tenure of property, including its origin, length of lease and other conditions under which the lease was held. Title deeds often include papers from the eighteenth and early nineteenth centuries which recite names of people formerly associated with the property. Testamentary papers include wills and other testamentary material which should prove to be useful to research of a genealogical nature.

There are three indexes which can be used to identify documents likely to be of interest to researchers:

- alphabetical index by name of estate,
- numerical index by record number,
- numerical index by box number.

The *Guide to Landed Estate Records* in PRONI contains an index to the Land Registry papers.

REGISTRY OF DEEDS

The Registry of Deeds was established by an Act of Parliament in 1708. The aim of the Act was to provide one central office in Dublin 'for the public registering of all deeds, conveyances and wills, that shall be made of any honours, manors, lands, tenements or hereditaments'. Researchers must remember that the Act establishing the Registry of Deeds had its origin in the Penal Laws. From 1704 to 1780 no Catholic could purchase a lease for more than thirty-one years nor could a Catholic invest in mortgages. Also landowners were often apathetic about officially registering leases with their tenants, particularly those on smallholdings.

The deeds registered include leases, mortgages, marriage settlements and wills. This can provide the researcher with names, addresses and occupations of the parties involved as well as the names of those who acted as witnesses. During registration, which often took place years after the original transaction, a summary of the deed called a memorial was made. The details of the memorial were then copied into a large bound volume. It is these transcript volumes that are available for public inspection.

Each deed registered was given its own individual reference number. In the indexes to the deeds the volume and the page are also given. For example, the reference 18.236.8764 means that this particular deed is on page 236 of volume 18 and is deed number 8764. This referencing system was used until 1832. After that the reference number includes the year in which the deed was registered.

Two indexes are available to the researcher: the Index of Grantors and the Lands Index. The format of the Index of Grantors has changed over the years. Before 1832 it gives the surname and the Christian name of the grantor, the surname of the grantee and the reference number. There is no indication of the location of the property concerned. After 1832 the Index of Grantors is more detailed and includes the county in which the property is located.

The Lands Index is arranged by county, with one or more counties per volume: the entries are arranged alphabetically, but only with regard to initial letter. Each entry gives the surnames of the parties, the name of the denomination of land and the reference number. After 1828 the Lands Index is subdivided by barony. Additional references were often put at the end of books.

The Registry of Deeds is located in a large Georgian building in Henrietta Street, Dublin. The main entrance for vehicles is off Constitution Hill. The Registry is open Monday to Friday, 10.00 am to 4.30 pm, and a small fee is charged for accessing the records. A member of staff will be on hand to offer help and advice. Although the layout of the building can be confusing, the arrangement of the records somewhat haphazard and the transcript volumes heavy and cumbersome, the Registry of Deeds is unlike any other archive in Ireland and is well worth a visit.

The Index of Grantors and the Lands Index are available on microfilm at the NLI, and PRONI has microfilms of both the indexes and the deeds (MIC/7 and MIC/311). A good guide to the Registry of Deeds is Jean Agnew's 'How to Use the Registry of Deeds', *Familia*, 2/6 (1990).

H

LAND AND VALUATION RECORDS

TITHE APPLOTMENT BOOKS

The tithe applotment books are unique records giving details of land occupation and valuations for individual holdings prior to the devastation brought about by the Great Famine and the resulting mass emigration. They list the occupiers of tithable land, not householders, as is the case in a census. Therefore, landless labourers and weavers were omitted, in addition to all purely urban dwellers.

The NAI holds manuscript books for almost every parish in the twenty-six counties of the Republic of Ireland (more than 2,000 in total), giving the names of the occupiers, the amount of land held and the sums to be paid in tithes. They are also available on microfilm at the NLI and the Gilbert Library in Dublin. More than 270 volumes were sent to PRONI for parishes in Cos. Antrim, Armagh, Cavan, Down, Fermanagh, Londonderry and Tyrone.

The researcher can face problems in using the tithe books. In some areas, for example, the land was of such poor quality that no tithe could be levied. Other areas were tithe-free for other reasons, usually because the church owned the land outright. Another more serious complication is that the subsequent dividing up and renaming of townlands, and the transfer of townlands from one parish to another and even from one county to another, is the cause of some confusion.

The Householders' Index, available on the shelves of the Public Search Room at PRONI and the NAI, can be used as a guide to the surnames listed in the tithe applotment books.

An index to the tithe applotment books is available on CD-ROM from Heritage World, The Heritage Centre, 26 Market Square, Dungannon, Co. Tyrone BT70 1AB.

VALUATION RECORDS

The levying of a rate in Ireland, to raise money to meet the costs of local government, dates from 1635. An Act of that year gave Justices of the Peace power to levy certain sums, known as the county cess or grand jury cess, upon the inhabitants of a local area for the execution of public works such as roads and bridges. By 1824, Parliament recognized the need for a more equitable method of measuring liability for cess and rates. The First Valuation Act was introduced in 1826 and a valuation of the whole of Ireland was prepared.

The townland valuation of the 1830s

Though often dismissed as being of fairly limited genealogical value, the townland valuation carried out in the 1830s can be an important source for those searching for their ancestors, particularly if those ancestors were urban dwellers. The records consist of manuscript field books (more than 4,500) compiled by parish, and describe each townland in the parish; the quality of the soil, and its valuations. Although the townland valuation was primarily concerned with the agricultural value of land, it also included details on houses valued at £3 or over (in 1838 this was raised to £5 or over but by this time most of Ulster had been surveyed). In the rural areas the names of only a few householders are given, and these tend to be of the gentry or the better class of tenant farmer. In towns, however, many more houses were substantial enough to reach the valuation, with the result that a large number of householders are recorded.

A set of field books for most parishes in Northern Ireland (except for Co. Tyrone) and for the Republic is available in the NAI under the reference OL5. Those for Northern Ireland are available at PRONI (VAL/1B); the accompanying annotated maps are listed under VAL/1A and VAL/1D.

Unfortunately, major towns and villages are not listed separately, but under the parish and barony in which they are located. In order to find the appropriate volume it is necessary to identify the parish. This can be done by consulting the *Alphabetical Index to the Townlands and Towns, Parishes and Baronies of Ireland*, which is available on the shelves of the Public Search Room at PRONI and the NAI. It is simply a matter of locating the relevant town and then running a finger along the columns listing the barony, parish, and poor law union.

The first general valuation (Griffith), 1848–1864

The 1848–64 valuation gives a complete list of occupiers of land, tenements and houses. This Primary Valuation of Ireland, better known as Griffith's Valuation, was to determine the amount of tax, or rates, each person should pay towards the support of the poor and destitute within each poor law union. The value of all privately held lands and buildings in both rural and urban areas was determined according to the rate at which each property could be rented year after year. The tax was fixed at about 6 per cent (with variations), for every pound of the rent value. Griffith's Valuation is arranged by county, within counties by poor law union division, and within unions by parish. It includes the following information: the name of the townland; the name of the householder or leaseholder; the name of the person from whom the property was leased; a description of the property; its acreage; and finally the valuation of the land and buildings.

The published version of Griffith's Valuation was based on the valuers' notebooks. It did not, however, include all the information provided by the notebooks, and some entries in a later published version have been updated. Earlier surveys were not included. PRONI has, for example, 59 manuscript volumes containing the valuation of Antrim, 1939, Cavan, 1841, and Down, 1839. A valuation of the City of Armagh was published in 1839. It contains the name and annual value of every holding in the city. A copy is available at the Irish Studies Library, Armagh, and the NLI. County and city libraries will normally hold those volumes relating to their localities.

Griffith's Valuation is of particular interest to anyone wishing to trace their family tree, because so little of the nineteenth-century census returns has survived. It is especially important for identifying emigrants' precise place of origin during this period. Emigration statistics point to the fact that a large proportion of the mass emigration that took place as result of the Great Famine of 1845–51 did not occur until after 1855, by which time the valuation was largely complete for the south and west of the country.

Family historians should be aware that Griffith's Valuation has some limitations. Partnership farms held under the rundale system had their individual parcels bracketed together without being separately measured, thereby excluding certain tenant names.

The NAI holds the original valuation surveyors' notebooks for the twenty-six counties of the Republic of Ireland. Those for parts of Co. Carlow, and for the Unions of Abbeyleix and Birr, Co. Tipperary, are missing. The notebooks consist of 'field books', 'house books' and 'tenure books'. All of these record a map reference for the holdings to which they relate. Of particular interest to the family historian are the house books, which record the occupier's name and the measurements of any buildings on their holdings. The tenure books give details of the annual rent paid and the year of any lease, which can be useful when searching estate papers of the Registry of Deeds.

The original notebooks for Northern Ireland are available at PRONI (VAL/2B). The valuers' annotated set of Ordnance Survey maps showing the location of every property is also available at PRONI (VAL/2A).

Printed editions of Griffith's Valuation are available in the public search rooms of the NAI and PRONI and at major libraries throughout Ireland. These volumes are arranged by poor law union, within union by county, and then subdivided into parishes and townlands. There is an index at the front of each volume which enables searchers to identify the page or pages in which a specific townland may be found.

An index to Griffith's Valuation for all of Ireland is available on CD-ROM from the American Genealogical Publishing Company. A CD-ROM set comprising page scans of the printed Griffith's Valuation has also been produced by Irish Microfilms Media Ltd in Dublin.

Valuation revisions

Another set of useful records are the 'cancelled land books' and 'current land books', which give details of all changes in the holdings from the time of Griffith's Valuation to the present day. When a change of occupancy occurred, the name of the lessee or householder was crossed off and the new owner's name written above it, while the year was noted on the right-hand side of the page. This helps to establish significant dates in family history, such as dates of death, sale or emigration. By the closing years of the nineteenth century most of the occupiers of land had become landowners, thanks to a series of Land Purchase Acts. This explains the initials L.A.P. (Land Act Purchase) that may be found stamped on an entry in the revision lists.

These volumes are arranged by poor law union within counties, and then subdivided into parishes and townlands. There is an index at the front of each volume which enables searchers to identify the page or pages in which a specific townland may be found. The Householders' Index can be used as a guide to the surnames listed in Griffith's Valuation.

The Valuation Office at the Irish Life Centre, Abbey Street Lower, Dublin 1, holds the cancelled land books for the Republic of Ireland. PRONI holds those for Northern Ireland (VAL/12B). The corresponding maps are also available at PRONI (VAL/12D).

The Landowners in Ireland: Return of Owners of Land of One Acre and Upwards, based on the findings of Griffith's Valuation, records more than 32,000 owners of land in Ireland in 1876, identifying them by province and county. It is available on the shelves of the Public Search Room at PRONI, the NAI and at major libraries.

I

CHURCH RECORDS

CHURCH OF IRELAND RECORDS

Parish registers of baptism, marriage and burial are the most important class of parish record available to researchers. They should not be neglected because an ancestor was of another denomination. Before 1782 it was not legal for Presbyterian ministers to perform marriages, and until 1844 they could not perform 'mixed marriages'. For this reason many marriages of other denominations, especially those classed as dissenters, are recorded in the Church of Ireland registers.

Under the Public Records Act 1867, an amendment of 1875 and the Parochial Records Act 1876, Church of Ireland parish registers of marriages prior to 1845 and of baptisms and burials prior to 1871 were declared to be public records. However, registers could be retained in parochial custody if an adequate place of storage was available. Almost half of the surviving registers held in Dublin were destroyed in 1922 and others have been lost at earlier periods. However, much of the lost information survives in transcripts and abstracts. The registers of 637 parishes in local custody survived, and in addition transcripts of or extracts from destroyed registers are available.

The NAI is in the process of completing the making of microfilm copies of surviving Church of Ireland parish registers, but not all of these are yet accessible to the public. PRONI holds microfilm copies of nearly all surviving registers for Northern Ireland. A growing number of surviving original registers is in the Representative Church Body Library in Dublin while others remain in local parochial custody.

The standard, but by no means complete, guide is the NAI 'Guide to Parochial Records of the Church of Ireland' (typescript), a partly updated version of which is *A Table of Church of Ireland Parochial Records and Copies*, edited by Noel Reid (Naas, 1994). See also *An Irish Genealogical Source: Guide to Church Records* (Belfast, 1974). For further information see Raymond Refausse 'Records of the Church of Ireland', in *Irish Church Records*, edited by J G Ryan (Dublin, 1992). John Granham lists surviving records parish-by-parish at www.ireland.com/ancestor/browse/counties/index.htm/

Marriage licence bonds

The prerogative and consistorial or diocesan courts could issue marriage licences to those who did not wish to pursue the method of having banns called. The original marriage licences and accompanying bonds were destroyed in 1922, but the prerogative and diocesan indexes to the bonds have survived, and for convenience are shelved with the testamentary indexes at the NAI. The *Betham Abstracts* contain details of prerogative marriage licences 1629–1801 and of Dublin Diocese marriage licences 1660–1824. Abstracts of Killaloe Diocese licences are held in the Genealogical Office, and abstracts of Ossory Diocese licences in the Representative Church Body Library. From 1845 the state registered non-Catholic marriages, and from 1864 marriages of all denominations were registered. PRONI also holds indices to the marriage licence bonds.

ROMAN CATHOLIC RECORDS

Roman Catholic parishes are often made up of parts of more than one civil parish. Also, most Roman Catholic parishes have more than one church. Sometimes only one register was kept for the entire parish, but at other times each church had its own register. Starting dates for Roman Catholic parish records vary from one part of the country to the other. They start earliest in the cities, with those for some city parishes in Dublin, Galway, Waterford, Cork and Limerick dating back to the late eighteenth century. Many of the registers in rural districts in the west of Ireland do not begin until the middle of the nineteenth century.

The main information given in baptism records is date, names of both parents (including the mother's maiden name, a custom not followed by Church of Ireland records), the names of two sponsors or godparents (often grandparents or other relatives) and sometimes (not always, alas) the place of abode (which is very useful when trying to locate individual families with a name common in the district). Illegitimate births are faithfully recorded.

The main information given in marriage records is date of marriage, place (the church in which the ceremony took place), names of both parties (including the bride's maiden name) and the names of two witnesses (often parents or other family, or best friends). The abode of the couple's parents is not always given. The latter situation improves in the 1860s with the introduction of new registers which have a column for address. Some priests had been careful to record addresses before this, but in general this is not the case. The same goes for baptism records.

Death or burial records were not well kept in Catholic parishes. The same register was generally used for births, marriages and deaths. Church of Ireland records of deaths and burials are much more thorough and extensive.

The registers remain the property of the Roman Catholic Church. Most of them are on microfilm (to 1880) at the NLI. Few of these are indexed. The NLI has produced a list of the parish registers which can be consulted on microfilm in the library. Parishes are listed alphabetically by diocese and the dates of the registers in each parish and the NLI call number are given. Please note that call numbers are not given for the Diocese of Cashel and Emly or for the Diocese of Kerry. This is because permission from the diocese is needed to view the films of these registers.

PRONI has microfilm copies for parishes in Ulster (MIC/1D, with some copies under CR/2).

PRESBYTERIAN RECORDS

Each Presbyterian congregation kept registers of baptisms and marriages: in general, they start later than those of the Church of Ireland. Additional Presbyterian records available for consultation at PRONI include session books, communicants' rolls and lists of members who emigrated. Because Presbyterians rarely kept burial registers, gravestone inscriptions provide valuable information that cannot be found elsewhere. It is also worth looking at Church of Ireland registers for baptisms, marriages and burials involving Presbyterians.

Another feature of Presbyterianism is the number of places that have more than one Presbyterian church, referred to as 1st, 2nd and 3rd. This, together with the fact that congregations tended to split or secede, makes life somewhat difficult for the researcher. Copies of some Presbyterian records are available in PRONI (MIC/1P and CR/3).

The Non-Subscribing Presbyterian Church

The Non-Subscribing Presbyterian Church was formed in 1725 when a number of ministers and congregations refused to subscribe to the Westminster Confession of Faith, the statement of doctrine of the Presbyterian Church. Some of the early Non-Subscribing Presbyterian Church records, created before the split, are in fact Presbyterian records: for example, the early records of Scarva Street Presbyterian Church in Banbridge are to be found in Banbridge Non-Subscribing Presbyterian Church records. Non-Subscribing Presbyterian Church records can be found in PRONI (MIC/1B or CR/4).

The Reformed Presbyterian Church

The Covenanter or Reformed Presbyterian Church was composed of those who adhered most strongly to the Covenants of 1638 and 1643 and who rejected the Revolution Settlement of 1691 in Scotland. It was not until the latter part of the eighteenth century that congregations began to be organized and ministers were ordained. The earliest records begin mainly in the mid-nineteenth century, apart from some early nineteenth-century sessions for Cullybackey, Co. Antrim, and Drumolg, Co. Londonderry. Some have been copied by PRONI (MIC/1C and CR/5).

THE METHODIST CHURCH

The majority of Methodists had been members of the established church and they remained members of their own local churches. Therefore they continued to go to the parish church for the administration of marriages, burials and baptisms. In 1816 a split developed between the Primitive Wesleyan Methodists, who retained their links with the established church, and the Wesleyan Methodists, who allowed their ministers to administer baptisms.

The majority of Methodist baptism and marriage registers do not begin until the 1830s and 1845 respectively. There are very few Methodist burial registers, because Methodist churches rarely had their own burial grounds. An important record is a large volume of baptismal entries for Methodist churches throughout Ireland deriving from the administrative records of the Methodist Church in Ireland (PRONI MIC/429/1), which may have been the product of an attempt to compile a central register of baptisms. Although incomplete, it contains baptisms from 1815 to 1840 that often predate the existing baptismal registers of Methodist churches.

THE RELIGIOUS SOCIETY OF FRIENDS

From the beginning Quakers were among the best record-keepers. Records include registers of births, marriages and deaths, minutes of meetings, accounts of sufferings and charity papers. As a result, Quaker records contain a great deal of information about local affairs.

The records are divided between the Society of Friends Historical Library, Dublin, and the Quaker library at the Friends Meeting House, Railway Street, Lisburn, Co. Antrim. Records dating from the seventeenth century have been copied by PRONI (MIC/16).

THE MORAVIAN CHURCH

The Moravians had their origin in a pre-Reformation Protestant Church called the *Unitas Fratrum* or United Brethren, a Hussite movement which arose in Moravia and Bohemia in what is now the Czech Republic. Brought to Ireland by the preacher John Cennick, who was invited to Dublin in 1746, there were soon Moravian societies in most Ulster counties. From these sprang the congregations making up the Moravian Church in Ireland – Ballinderry, Kilwarlin, Cracehill, Cracefield, Belfast (University Road and Cliftonville) and Dublin. The Moravians had less impact outside the North and Dublin, but did establish some congregations in Cos. Galway and Clare.

Apart from baptism, marriages and burial registers, the Moravian Church also maintains very detailed membership registers, recording for each member date of birth, previous denomination, when deceased or left and the reason for leaving. Ministers' diaries contain births, marriages and deaths, the names of those who joined the church and those who left, and lists of members.

PRONI has copied all the records held at Gracehill Moravian church which comprise not only those for Gracehill but also those for other churches including the Dublin church (MIC/1F).

THE BAPTIST CHURCH

Baptists trace their origin from John Smyth (1554–1612), a Separatist exile in Amsterdam who, in 1609, reinstated the 'Baptism of conscious [adult] believers' and thereby reaffirmed his belief in the individual's responsibility for his or her soul. Although the Baptists were among the independent churches that came into Ireland in the mid-seventeenth century, it was the nineteenth century before they began to make progress in Ulster. The earliest records in PRONI's custody begin in the 1860s and consist of marriages and minute books. As the Baptist Church does not practise infant baptism, there are no baptism registers indicating births, but details of those who came into membership can be found in the minute books. The Baptists do not have any burial grounds, hence the absence of burial registers.

Baptist Church records remain in local custody or with the Baptist Union of Ireland, 117 Lisburn Road, Belfast. Family historians should contact either PRONI or check the local directory for the location and number of the relevant church.

CONGREGATIONAL CHURCH

Although the Congregationalists came to Ireland as early as the seventeenth century, few records exist before the 1880s. An exception to this rule are those of Richhill Congregational Church, whose baptismal records date from 1846 and lists of members from *c*.1848. These records are deposited in PRONI (CR/7/7).

HUGUENOT RECORDS

The original Huguenot registers were lost in the mid–nineteenth century and all subsequent efforts to trace them have failed. The Huguenot Society of Great Britain and Ireland was established in 1885 to collect and publish information relating to the history and genealogy of Huguenots. The Huguenot Library at University College, Gower Street, London

WC1, contains much material on Irish Huguenot families not available elsewhere, including manuscripts, pedigrees and collections of family papers.

An Irish section of the society was established in 1987. All members of the Society receive a copy of *Huguenot Proceedings*, a useful work of reference for the family historian. An Annual General Meeting is held in Ireland each year and a church service, in St Patrick's Cathedral, Dublin, is held each November. Most Huguenots conformed, in due course, to the Church of Ireland. For this reason, the Irish section of the Huguenot Society has placed its archive in the Representative Church Body Library in Dublin.

JEWISH RECORDS
The Irish Jewish Museum is located in Portobello, around South Circular Road, Dublin 8. The former Walworth Road Synagogue there fell into disuse and ceased to function in the mid-1970s. The premises remained locked for almost ten years and were brought back to life again with the establishment of the Irish Jewish Museum Committee in late 1984. The museum contains a substantial collection of memorabilia relating to the Irish Jewish communities and their various associations and contributions to present-day Ireland. The material relates to the last 150 years and is associated with the communities of Belfast, Cork, Derry, Dublin, Limerick and Waterford.

7

POOR LAW RECORDS

The Boards of Guardians kept comprehensive records throughout the nineteenth century. Of all the records, the registers of admission and discharge are the most valuable. Unfortunately, the registers have not survived as well as other poor law union records. Of all the classes, the minute books are probably the best survivors. They contain miscellaneous information about the administration of the poor law unions, and often include details of staff employed by the poor law union.

The county libraries of Cavan, Donegal, Galway, Kerry, Kildare, Kilkenny, Laois, Leitrim, Louth, Meath, Offaly, Sligo and the Tipperary joint libraries all have poor law union records, in particular, board of guardians' minute books. Addresses, and in some cases further details, will be found in the *Directory of Irish Archives*. The county council archives of Mayo, Roscommon, Waterford and Wicklow also hold poor law union records.

Other archives which have poor law union records are:

- Monaghan County Museum, which holds the records of Castleblayney workhouse;
- Limerick Regional Archives, which holds records for Counties Clare, Limerick and Tipperary;
- Cork Archives Institute;
- The de Valera Library and Museum in Ennis, Co. Clare, which holds poor law union records relating to County Clare.

The NAI also has a good collection, which contains a large quantity of Co. Dublin poor law union material. They have the minutes of the boards of guardians for the North and South Dublin Unions extending from 1840 to 1920. In 1920 the two unions were merged and the records of the united unions are available to 1938. The registers of admissions and discharges from these workhouses are available from 1840 to 1920.

The NAI also has similar records for the Rathdown Union, which covered parts of north Co. Wicklow and south Co. Dublin for the period 1839 to 1955. Records, mainly Board of Guardians' minute books, for Balrothery Union, Co. Dublin, Bawnboy Union, Co. Cavan, and Lismore Union, Co. Waterford, are also held.

The NLI holds the board of guardians' minute books for the Mayo unions of Ballina, Ballinrobe, Belmullet, Castlebar, Claremorris, Killala, Newport, Swinford and Westport. It also has a number of miscellaneous items such as a letter-book for Ennistymon Union and accounts for some of the above-mentioned Mayo unions.

The twenty-seven poor law unions in the counties of Northern Ireland are held by PRONI as follows:

- BG1 – Antrim, Co. Antrim
- BG2 – Armagh, Co. Armagh
- BG3 – Ballycastle, Co. Antrim
- BG4 – Ballymena, Co. Antrim
- BG5 – Ballymoney, Co. Antrim
- BG6 – Banbridge, Co. Down
- BG7 – Belfast, Co. Antrim and Co. Down
- BG8 – Castlederg, Co. Tyrone
- BG9 – Clogher, Co. Tyrone
- BG10 – Coleraine, Co. Londonderry
- BG11 – Cookstown, Co. Tyrone
- BG12 – Downpatrick, Co. Down
- BG13 – Dungannon, Co. Tyrone
- BG14 – Enniskillen, Co. Fermanagh
- BG15 – Irvinestown, Co. Fermanagh
- BG16 – Kilkeel, Co. Down
- BG17 – Larne, Co. Antrim
- BG18 – [Newton] Limavady, Co. Londonderry

- BG19 – Lisburn, Co. Antrim
- BG20 – Lisnaskea, Co. Fermanagh
- BG21 – Londonderry, Co. Londonderry
- BG22 – Lurgan, Co. Armagh
- BG23 – Magherafelt, Co. Londonderry
- BG24 – Newry, Co. Down
- BG25 – Newtownards, Co. Down
- BG26 – Omagh, Co. Tyrone
- BG27 – Strabane, Co. Tyrone
- BG28 – Gortin, Co. Tyrone (united to Omagh *c.*1870)

For details of the records which have survived for each union, researchers should consult the grey calendars, which are available on the shelves of the Public Search Room.

K

RECORDS IN BRITAIN

CENSUS RETURNS

A census was taken in Britain every ten years after 1801 (except during the Second World War). Until 1841 the census was basically a headcount of the numbers of people (male and female), houses and families in a parish or township. From 1841 the census lists the names of everyone in the house, the address, approximate ages and occupations.

In 1841 those born in Ireland are recorded simply with the initial 'I' after their names. Later censuses are little better: entries for place of birth often simply state 'Ireland', although the name of a county or large town is sometimes given. In Scotland, from 1851, the specific town or parish of birth is given. Gravestone inscriptions and death notices in newspapers will probably provide the best means of identifying a more precise Irish address of an ancestor.

The original census returns for 1841–91 for England, Wales, the Channel Islands and the Isle of Man are kept in the National Archives, in London. However, those for your particular county should also be available in the local record office. The 1901 census for England and Wales is available online at www.1901census.nationalarchives.gov.uk

The 1851, 1861, 1871, 1881 and 1891 census returns hosted by www.ancestry.co.uk can be searched for free. For a fee images of the returns can be downloaded.

At the time of writing the 1911 census is being digitized and it is expected that it will be released in 2009.

In Scotland there has been a census every ten years since 1801 (excluding 1941) but only those returns after 1841 (with a few earlier exceptions) carry details of named residents. Census returns for 1841–1901 can be consulted at the General Register Office in Edinburgh. Copies on microfilm may be consulted in LDS Family History Centres around the world. LDS centres also carry microfiche indexes to the 1881 census returns. Computerized indexes for the 1861, 1871, 1881, 1891 and 1901 censuses are available at the General Register Office in Edinburgh, and also online (for a fee) at www.scotlandspeople.gov.uk (includes images of the 1861, 1871, 1891 and 1901 censuses, and full transcript of 1881).

WILLS

The prerogative court of Canterbury may have proved the wills of Irish people, usually the wealthier sort, who died with goods in England before 1858. These are held by the National Archives, London. Digital images of the wills are available online – it is possible to search for the will and download it for a small fee (see www.nationalarchives.gov.uk/documentsonline/wills.asp). After 1858 wills would have been proved centrally at the Principal Probate Registry. Searches can be made there: indexes covering the period to 1943 are also on microfiche at many archives and Mormon FHCs.

In Scotland it was more common for people to make testaments dealing solely with moveable goods. These were proved by local commissary courts under the Principal Commissariot of Edinburgh. From 1824 testaments were proved in county sheriffs' courts. All documents 1513–1901 are viewable (www.scotlandspeople.gov.uk) and can be downloaded for a small fee.

SERVICEMEN

Of course, many Irishmen served in the British Army and the Navy, and these records can be explored at the National Archives, London. It is important that you know when your ancestor was in the forces and the regiment or unit with which they served. For the nineteenth century the National Archives, London, has several series of records detailing the service of officers and an alphabetical card index to these records is available. Collections include:

- Correspondence about the sale and purchase of commissions between 1793 and 1871 (WO 31): contains a great deal of valuable genealogical information.
- Records of military commissions and appointments of Irish officers between 1768 and 1877 (HO 123).
- Information on ancestors who served in the rank and file (WO 97).
- Records relating to the Army in Ireland, 1775–1923 (WO 35).
- Muster rolls of the Irish militia, 1793–1876 (WO 13).
- The Royal Kilmainham Hospital acted as a hospital for disabled soldiers (known as in-pensioners) and distributed money to out-pensioners: registers of in- and out-pensioners in the admission books, 1704–1922 (WO118), and discharge documents, 1783–1822 (WO119).
- Other Irish soldiers and sailors had their pensions paid by the Royal Chelsea Hospital or by Greenwich Hospital in London, 1842–62 (WO 22/141–205) and 1882–3 (WO 22/209–25). They can be used to trace changes of residence and dates of death.
- The only separate naval records for Irishmen are of nominations to serve in the Irish Coastguard, 1821–49 (ADM 175/99–100).

For a more complete introduction see Simon Fowler's *Tracing Your Army Ancestors* (Pen & Sword Books, 2006) and *Army Service Records of the First World War* (Countryside Books, 2003).

BIRTHS, MARRIAGES AND DEATHS

Civil registration of births, marriages and deaths began in England and Wales in 1837 and in Scotland in 1855. These can be consulted at county record offices. The National Archives, London, holds the union indexes of births, marriages and deaths registered officially in England and Wales from 1 July 1837. These are called union indexes because registration districts took their name from the poor law union in which they were based. You can search the indexes online for a small fee (at www.findmypast.com).

The indexes to Scottish registers of births, marriages and deaths since 1 January 1855 and of births and marriages in the Church of Scotland from about 1553 are held at the Scottish General Register Office. There is also a computerized link to these records at the National Archives, London, or you can search online at www.scotlandspeople.gov.uk and view indexes of birth registrations (1855–1906), marriages (1855–1931) and deaths (1855–1956), again for a small fee.

Those wishing to trace baptismal or marriage records from before July 1837 should consult the International Genealogical Index, known as the IGI. This is an index to births, baptisms and marriages worldwide, although coverage is not complete. The indexes to the British Isles cover the period from the beginning of registration to 1875. The indexes for England and Wales are mainly to Church of England parish registers and to nearly all the registers in RG4 in the National Archives.

L

EMIGRATION RECORDS

RESEARCH IN THE UNITED STATES

Passenger lists

The USA has comprehensive passenger lists for ships arriving from 1820, but they provide only two clues relating to the origin of the emigrant: the port of departure of the ship and the nationality of the passenger. This is of limited value when it is realized that the vast majority of Irish emigrants in the nineteenth century sailed from Liverpool. It was not until 1893 and the Immigration Act that the former address in Ireland of an emigrant was recorded.

Numerous passenger lists have been published in books and on CD-ROM or on the internet. Many of these can be found at the library of the Society of Genealogists, and at PRONI, NAI and NLI. *The Famine Immigrants: Irish Immigrants Arriving at the Port of New York, 1846–1851*, by I A Glazier and M Tepper, contains an impressive 650,000 names. B Mitchell has produced a number of books, including *Irish Passenger Lists, 1803–06: Lists of Passengers Sailing from Ireland to America Extracted from the Hardwick Papers* (GPC, 1995) and *Irish Passenger Lists, 1847–71: Lists of Passengers Sailing from Londonderry to America on Ships of the J & J Cooke Line & the McCorkell Line* (GPC, 1988).

An invaluable website containing a number of lists is run by the American Immigrant Ship Transcription Guild (www.istg.rootsweb.com). The website www.genealogybranches.com/irishpassengerlists is perhaps the best overall guide to passenger ships between Ireland and the United States. Also check the American Family History Immigration History Centre Ellis Island website, an online database of 22 million passengers and crew members who went through Ellis Island (New York), for the period 1892 to 1924 (www.ellisislandrecords.org). The websites www.ancestry.com and www.genealogy.com also have indexes listing millions of Irish immigrants to America.

Census records

A census has been taken every ten years in the USA since 1790, and from 1850 the returns provide the country of birth and age of all members of the household, not just the head of household. Sometimes the census enumerator has recorded more specific information than just the country of birth. Those before 1930 are searchable online at www.ancestry.com (with 1880 free at www.familysearch.org).

Many state censuses also exist. These were generally taken between federal censuses and contain information similar to that found in the federal censuses.

Birth, death and marriage certificates

These may help to pinpoint your immigrant ancestor's origins if he or she married or died in the United States. Although the quality of information held on death certificates varies according to where they were filed, they may give the exact birthdate, the age in years and the birthplace, which may be the townland, city, parish, county or just 'Ireland'.

If your Irish ancestor married in the United States, the marriage certificate might identify where the bride and/or groom was born in Ireland and perhaps even their ages. Parents' names are often listed. Birth, marriage and death certificates of children may also help identify where their parents where born.

The United States has no national registry of births, marriages and deaths. Such records are held locally by either the county or state. The best sources are www.cyndislist.com arranged by state, and A Eakle and J Cerny, *The Source: A Guidebook of American Genealogy*, new edn, 1996, by L. Szucs and S. Luebking. Some civil registration is becoming available (www.ancestry.com). You can also write to the appropriate government office to order a copy of a birth, marriage or death certificate. The

US Department of Health and Human Services publishes a list of current addresses and fees in a booklet entitled *Where to Write for Vital Records*. You can also search birth, marriage and death indexes for many states (www.ancestry.com).

RESEARCH IN CANADA

Census records

The earliest major census of Canada was taken in 1666 in the area which later became Quebec. The names, ages and occupations of all men, women and children were recorded parish by parish. Of particular interest are the censuses taken after 1851, which name the entire household, with age, occupation, birthplace, religion, martial status, gender, race and other details listed for each person. Hundreds of districts of the 1901 census have been indexed and are searchable (www.ancestry.com).

The Church of the Latter-Day Saints (Mormons) has indexed the 1881 Canadian census. This index contains 4.3 million names and may be searched online (www.familysearch.org).

Library and Archives Canada has posted digital images of the 1901 and 1911 censuses on the Canadian Genealogy Centre website (www. genealgy.gc.ca). The Ontario Genealogical Society has published a head-of-household index to the 1871 returns for Ontario.

Passenger lists

In 1895, after it was noted that 40 per cent of all passengers arriving in Canada were actually bound for the USA, a system of joint inspection of immigrants coming 'overland' from Canada was established. From 1847, the two ports of Portland and Falmouth, Maine, were becoming increasingly popular as ports of entry for Irish immigrants coming down from Quebec and the Maritime Provinces to the USA. In these cases, therefore, Irish immigrants leaving Canada for the USA will be noted.

Few passenger lists survive for vessels arriving in Canada before 1865. The Family History Library (Mormon Church) has microfilms of surviving passenger lists for Quebec, 1865–1900, and Halifax, 1881–99.

Birth, death and marriage records

In the absence of passenger lists the best hope of linking an ancestor to their place of origin in Ireland may lie in the identification of a marriage entry for a newly arrived immigrant in a church register. Frequently, the marriage registers give the county of birth in Ireland, and occasionally the exact place of origin of bride and groom. In the years 1801 to 1845, for example, the weddings of 3,000 Irish immigrants, with parents' names and native parishes, were recorded in Halifax, Nova Scotia.

Civil registration in Canada started at different times in each individual province as follows: Nova Scotia, 1864; Ontario, 1869; British Columbia, 1872; Saskatchewan, 1878; Manitoba, 1882; New Brunswick, 1888; Newfoundland, 1891; Alberta, 1897; Prince Edward Island, 1906; Yukon and Northwest Territories, 1896; and Quebec, 1926. Records are held by the provincial Registrars General and, apart from Quebec, access is usually only by application. See www.cyndislist.com under each province; www.ancestry.com now has some Ontario and British Columbia civil registration online.

Land grants

Land grants can be extremely useful in identifying recent immigrants. To obtain land from the colonial government, and after 1867 from the provincial authorities, a settler had to make a formal application, known as a petition, in which details on place of origin, date of arrival in Canada, names of wife and children and their ages are often given. There is a computerized Land Records Index for the years 1780 to 1914 with two alphabetical listings, one by applicant's name and one by township.

RESEARCHING IN AUSTRALIA

Australia has a superb collection of records for the genealogically minded. The three prime sources of convict records, assisted immigration lists and birth, marriage and death certificates provide a wealth of relevant detail for those tracking down their Irish ancestors.

Census records

A number of census records from the nineteenth century were lost in a major fire, and none from the twentieth century have been retained, apparently for reasons of protection of privacy, and a fear that failure to protect privacy would put the accuracy of the census in doubt. Early census records have survived for each of the states as follows:

New South Wales
Records date back to the original convict 'return' of 1788, which was essentially the earliest Australian census, including people on Norfolk Island. There are censuses from 1828, 1841 (available online at www. records.nsw.gov.au/), 1891 and 1901 (the latter was destroyed, but in both cases collectors' notebooks have survived).

South Australia
South Australia was part of New South Wales until 1836, which means records before that come under New South Wales. The census of 1841 has survived, and can be seen online (www.jaunay.com/1841.census.html, with all the names listed at www.jaunay.com.census.html).

Tasmania
Tasmania (originally called Van Diemen's Land) was part of New South Wales until 1825, and so most early records come under that. Many musters, the earliest from 1803, have been published, and you can find the complete census records up to 1857 at the Archives Office of Tasmania (www.archives.tas.gov.au/).

Victoria
It was only in 1851 that Victoria separated from New South Wales. This means that many records before this come under New South Wales. However, you can find convict returns for 1825 and 1828, after which there are four separate census returns going to 1844, all of which can be seen in the Public Records Office of Victoria (www.prov.vic.gov.au/).

Western Australia
The first Western Australia record is the 1829 Swan River muster, after which you can find the returns from four censuses, the last of which was taken in 1859. Records are in either the State Archives (www.sro.wa.gov.au/) or the Battye Library (www.liswa.wa.gov.au/battye.html).

Northern Territories
The Northern Territories were part of South Australia from 1863 to 1911, after which they became a Commonwealth Territory. The censuses of 1881 and 1891 are available in the National Archives (www.naa.gov.au/).

Passenger lists

Passenger lists document the movement of people into and out of Australia. The master of each passenger vessel and aircraft arriving in, or departing from, Australian ports was required to provide the authorities with a list of passengers disembarking and embarking from that port. Depending on the port, passenger lists and crew records are deposited at the state capitals: Hobart, Sydney, Canberra and Perth. Passenger lists are publicly available once they are more than thirty years old.

The National Archives are responsible for records of the Commonwealth government of Australia. The Commonwealth government assumed responsibility for passenger arrivals and departures in 1923, so its holdings date mostly from 1924, although it does hold some records dating back to the 1850s. Unfortunately, there are no comprehensive name indexes for passenger records. To search for family members effectively, it is necessary to know the year, month and the port or state where they landed. Passengers were listed under each ship so knowing the ship's name is also useful when searching these records. If you are unable to identify the date of arrival within two months, your search could be very time-consuming.

Transportation records

The transportation of convicts to Australia came about as a result of the British government's problems coping with an eighteenth-century crime wave at home that threatened to overwhelm the inadequate prison system. A number of Irish records on convicts have been microfilmed and indexed by name and can be searched (www.nationalarchives.ie/topics/transportation/search01.html).

Births, deaths and marriages

These records are an invaluable source of information on the origins of Irish Australians. The Genealogical Society of Utah has published a CD-ROM collection entitled *Australian Vital Records Index, 1788–1905*, which indexes 4.8 million births, marriages and deaths in a number of locations (it may be purchased online at www.familyseach.org).

Researchers can search the civil registration of New South Wales online at www.bdm.nsw.gov.au for births, 1788–1905; deaths, 1788–1945; and marriages, 1788–1945.

Australasian Genealogical Computer Index

The Australasian Genealogical Computer Index is a microfiche collection of approximately two million records of cemetery transcriptions, newspaper articles, Irish transportation records and other material. It is available at the Family History Library and at a number of libraries in Australia.

RESEARCHING IN NEW ZEALAND

Passenger lists

Passenger lists in New Zealand, as in Australia, were kept at the port of arrival. Most official passenger lists are in the National Archives in Wellington but many other lists are held locally. The earliest are those for the New Zealand Company vessels, arriving at the ports of Wellington, Nelson, New Plymouth and Otago. These lists date from 1840 and provide the immigrant's name, age, occupation, wife's age and children's age and sex. From 1853, provincial governments at Canterbury, Wellington, Nelson, Auckland and Otago administered New Zealand. Each province compiled passenger lists of varying quality. The arrival of ships and passengers was reported in local newspapers and these are worth consulting for detailed accounts of the immigrants and their voyages.

Census records

The first full census in New Zealand was conducted in 1851, and the census was triennial until 1881, at which time it became five-yearly. Unfortunately, in both New Zealand and Australia, census records were destroyed once the relevant statistical information had been extracted from them.

Births, deaths and marriages

Civil registration of births and deaths began in 1848, but marriages were not recorded until 1855. In terms of identifying the Irish origins of an ancestor, death certificates are an extremely valuable source, especially after 1876. From that year the place of birth, the parents' names and the date and place of marriage of the deceased were recorded. Marriage certificates from 1880 are equally useful as they give the birthplace and parents' names for both bride and groom.

Access to all birth registers held at the New Zealand National Archives is restricted, but death and marriage registers held can be accessed. The complete registers of births, deaths and marriages are held by the Central Registry of Births, Deaths and Marriages, Department of Internal Affairs (www.bdm.govt.nz).

Parish records
Parish registers of baptisms, marriages and burials, held either by local clergy or, in the case of Presbyterian records, in their archives in Dunedin. These should be consulted for details on births, marriages and deaths before the commencement of civil registration. Most gravestones have been transcribed and are on microfilm at branches of the New Zealand Society of Genealogists.

SELECT BIBLIOGRAPHY

Bardon, Jonathan. *A History of Ulster* (Belfast, 1992)

Barnard, Toby. *A Guide to Sources for the History of Material Culture in Ireland, 1500–2000* (Dublin, 2005)

Bartlett, Tom, and Jeffrey, Keith (eds). *A Military History of Ireland* (Cambridge, 1996)

Beckett, J C. *The Making of Modern Ireland, 1603–1923* (London, 1966)

Begley, D F (ed.). *Irish Genealogy: A Record Finder* (Dublin, 1981)

Brynn, Edward. *Crown and Castle: British Rule in Ireland, 1800–1830* (Dublin, 1978)

Carleton, S T. *Heads and Hearths: The Hearth Money Rolls and Poll Tax Returns for Co. Antrim, 1660–69* (Belfast, 1991)

Christian, Peter. *The Genealogist's Internet* (London, 2001)

Clare, Revd W. *A Simple Guide to Irish Genealogy* (London, 1938)

Connolly, S J (ed.). *The Oxford Companion to Irish History* (Oxford, 1998)

Crawford, W H. 'The Significance of Landed Estates in Ulster 1600–1820', *Irish Economic and Social History*, 17 (1990)

Crawford, W H. 'The Ulster Irish in the Eighteenth Century', *Ulster Folklife*, 28 (1982)

Crawford, W H and Trainor, B. *Aspects of Irish Social History, 1750–1800* (Belfast, 1969)

De Breffny, Brian. *Irish Family Names: Arms, Origins and Locations* (Dublin, 1982)

Dickson, R J. *Ulster Emigration to Colonial America 1718–1775* (Belfast, 1966)

Dooley, T. *Sources for the History of Landed Estates in Ireland* (Dublin, 2000)

Fabricant, Carol. *Swift's Landscape* (London, 1982)

Falley, M D. *Irish and Scotch-Irish Ancestral Research* (Strasburg, VA, 1962)

Fowler, Simon. *Tracing Irish Ancestors* (London, 2001)

Fowler, Simon. *Tracing Your Army Ancestors* (Barnsley, 2006)

Gillespie, R G (ed.). *Settlement and Survival on an Ulster Estate* (Belfast, 1988)

Goldstrom, J M and Clarkson, L A. *Irish Population, Economy and Society* (Oxford, 1981)

Green, E R R (ed.). *Essays in Scotch-Irish History* (Belfast, 1969)

Grenham, J. *Tracing Your Irish Ancestors* (Dublin, 1992)

Hall, Mr and Mrs Samuel Carter. *Tour of Ireland 1840* (republ. London, 1984)

Hayward, Richard. *In Praise of Ulster* (Belfast, 1938)

Helferty, S and Refausse, R. *A Directory of Irish Archives*, 4th edn (Dublin, 2003)

Herber, Mark D. *Ancestor Trails: The Complete Guide to British Genealogy and Family History* (Stroud, 1997)

Hey, David. *The Oxford Companion to Local and Family History* (Oxford, 1996)

Howells, Cyndi. *Netting Your Ancestors: Genealogical Research on the Internet* (Baltimore, MD, 1999)

Kinealy, Christine. *Tracing Your Irish Roots* (Belfast, 1991)

Kinealy, Christine and Parkhill, Trevor (eds). *The Famine in Ulster* (Belfast, 1997)

Lucey, M. 'Rateable Valuation in Ireland', *Administration*, 12/1 (Spring 1964)

MacAtasney, G. *The Famine in Lurgan and Portadown* (Dublin, 1997)

McCarthy, T. *The Irish Roots Guide* (Dublin, 1991)

MacConghail, Maire and Gorry, Paul. *Tracing Your Irish Ancestors* (Glasgow, 1997)

MacCuarta, Brian (ed.). *Ulster 1641: Aspects of the Rising* (Belfast, 1993)

MacLysaght, E. *Irish Families: Their Names, Arms and Origins* (Dublin, 1957)

MacLysaght, E. 'Seventeenth Century Hearth Money Rolls', *Analecta Hibernica*, 24 (1967)

Maxwell, C. *Dublin under the Georges* (London, 1956)

Maxwell, C. *Country and Town under the Georges* (Dundalk, 1949)

Maxwell, I. *Tracing Your Ancestors in Northern Ireland* (Edinburgh, 1997)

Maxwell, I. *Researching Armagh Ancestors* (Belfast, 2000)

Maxwell, I. *Researching Down Ancestors* (Belfast, 2004)

Neill, K. *How to Trace Family History in Northern Ireland* (Belfast, 1986)

Nolan, W. *Tracing the Past* (Dublin, 1982)

Nolan, W (ed.). *The Shaping of Ireland: The Geographical Perspective* (Dublin, 1986)

Nowlan, K (ed.). *Travel and Transportation in Ireland* (Dublin, 1973)

O'Neill, Robert K. *Ulster Libraries: A Visitor's Guide* (Belfast, 1987)

O'Sullivan, Harold. 'The Magennis Lordship of Iveagh in the Early Modern Period, 1534 to 1691', in *Down: History and Society* (Dublin, 1997)

Ouimette, David S. *Finding Your Irish Ancestors: A Beginner's Guide* (Provo, UT, 2005)

Phair, P B. 'Guide to the Registry of Deeds', *Hibernica Analecta*, 23 (1966)

Proudfoot, Lindsay (ed.). *Down: History and Society* (Dublin, 1997)

Quinn, S E. *Trace Your Irish Ancestors* (Wicklow, 1989)

Radford, Dwight A and Betit, Kyle J. *A Genealogist's Guide to Discovering Your Irish Ancestors* (Cincinatti, OH, 2001)

Raymond, Stuart. *Irish Family History on the Web*, 2nd edn (Bury, 2004)

Robinson, Philip. *The Plantation of Ulster* (Belfast, 1994)

Ryan, J G. *Irish Records: Sources for Family and Local History* (Salt Lake City, UT, 1988)

Ryan, J G. *Irish Church Records* (Dublin, 1992)

Ryan, J G. *Sources for Irish Family History* (Dublin, 2001)

Thackeray, W M. *Irish Sketchbook* (1843; repr. Belfast, 1985)

Walker, Brian. *Ulster Politics: The Formative Years 1868–1886* (Belfast, 1989)

Young, A. *A Tour in Ireland, 1776–1779* (republ. Belfast, 1983)

INDEX